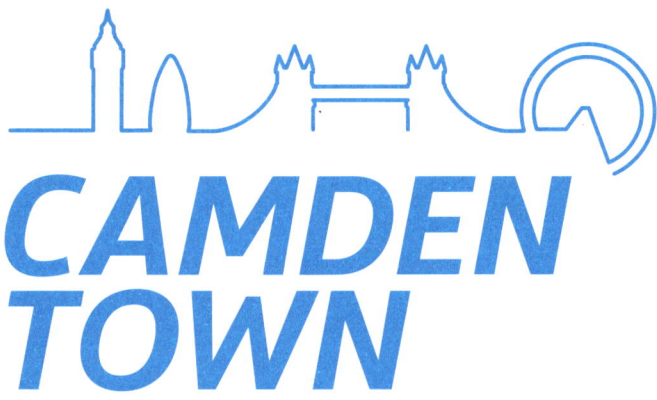

CAMDEN TOWN

Oberstufe

Arbeitsheft zu den Pflichtmaterialien

Erarbeitet von

Svenja Alpen-Kühne
Anne-Kathrin Böker
Svenja Kelly

Abkürzungen:

AE	American English	*infml.*	informal
BE	British English	*pl.*	plural
e.g.	exempli gratia (Latin) = for example	*sb*	somebody
i.e.	id est (Latin) = that is	*sth*	something

Webcodes
Auf manchen Seiten findest du Webcodes, die dich zu zusätzlichen Materialien im Internet führen.
Gib dazu einfach den Code auf www.westermann.de/webcode ins Suchfeld ein.

Filmauszüge
Je nach Abspielgerät und verwendeter Software kann es vorkommen, dass die Zeitangaben zu den
Filmauszügen nicht exakt mit den im Kapitel angegebenen übereinstimmen.

Behold the Dreamers
Die Verweise zu *Behold the Dreamers* beziehen sich auf die Ausgabe: Imbolo Mbue, *Behold the Dreamers*,
Westermann 2024, ISBN: 978-3-425-73073-8.

seven methods of killing kylie jenner
Die Verweise zu *seven methods of killing kylie jenner* beziehen sich auf diese Ausgabe, die bei
Westermann erhältlich ist: Jasmine Lee-Jones, *seven methods of killing kylie jenner*,
ISBN: 978-3-425-73070-7. Kostenlose Annotationen finden sich auf www.westermann.de.

Verweise auf *Skills pages* und *Workshops*
Die Verweise auf *Skills pages* und *Workshops* beziehen sich auf das Schulbuch *Camden Town Oberstufe
Qualifikationsphase Niedersachsen*, ISBN: 978-3-425-73642-6.

© 2024 Westermann Bildungsmedien Verlag GmbH, Georg-Westermann-Allee 66, 38104 Braunschweig
www.westermann.de

Druck A[1] / Jahr 2024
Alle Drucke der Serie A sind im Unterricht parallel verwendbar.

Redaktion: Isabel Klein, Schönau
Umschlaggestaltung: Gingco.Net Werbeagentur GmbH & Co. KG, Braunschweig
Layout: Visuelle Lebensfreude, Hannover; thom bahr GRAFIK, Mainz
Druck und Bindung: Westermann Druck GmbH, Georg-Westermann-Allee 66, 38104 Braunschweig

ISBN 978-3-425-**73699**-0

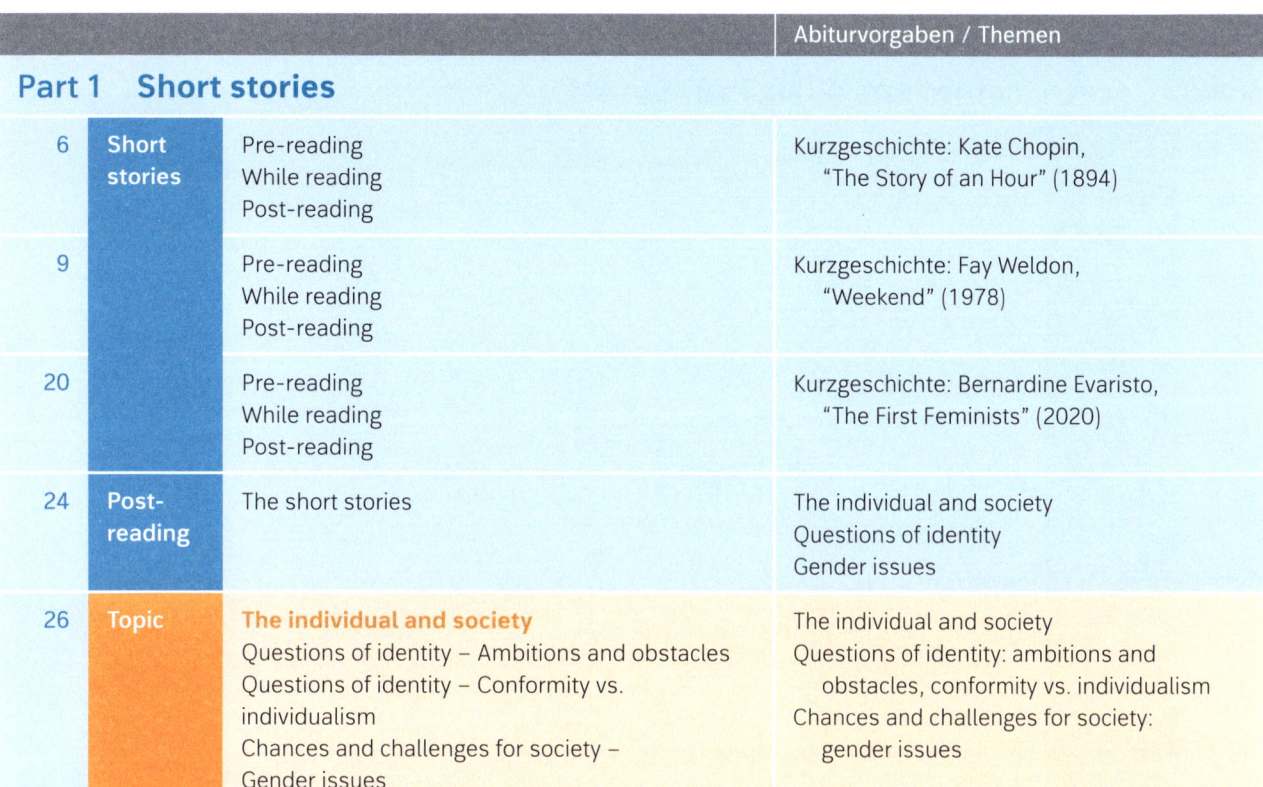

Contents

Liebe Schülerin, lieber Schüler,

mit diesem Arbeitsheft kannst du dich ideal auf das Abitur vorbereiten. Du beschäftigst dich mit allen Texten, die für das Abitur vorgeschrieben sind, und außerdem mit weiteren abiturrelevanten Themen.

Für das schriftliche Abitur 2026 müssen die folgenden Materialien unter den genannten inhaltlichen Gesichtspunkten behandelt werden:

Kurzprosa:

Kate Chopin, "The Story of an Hour" (1894)
Fay Weldon, "Weekend" (1978)
Bernardine Evaristo, "The First Feminists" (2020)
→ Themenfeldbezug: The individual and society
- Questions of identity: ambitions and obstacles, conformity vs. individualism
- Chances and challenges for society: gender issues

Roman:

Imbolo Mbue, *Behold the Dreamers* (2016)
→ Themenfeldbezug: Politics, culture, society – between tradition and change (Bezugskultur: USA)
- From past to present: American ideals and realities – freedom, equality and the pursuit of happiness
- Current issues: questions of identity, political, cultural and social developments

Kurzdrama:

Jasmine Lee-Jones, *seven methods of killing kylie jenner* (2019, Neubearbeitung 2021)
→ Themenfeldbezug: The media
- The changing media landscape: traditional and modern media
- The impact of the media on the individual and society: information, entertainment, manipulation

Aufbau des Arbeitsheftes

In jedem Kapitel erfolgt zunächst eine inhaltliche Sicherung und allgemeine Bearbeitung der jeweiligen Materialien. Auf speziell ausgewiesenen *Topic*-Seiten werden die Themenfeldbezüge generell eingeführt, bevor sie im Kontext der jeweiligen Materialien noch einmal vertieft werden. Wo es sich anbietet, werden auch weitere Themen aus dem Lehrplan (Kerncurriculum) aufgegriffen.

An vielen Stellen findest du Verweise auf *Skills pages* und *Workshops* im Schulbuch *Camden Town Oberstufe Qualifikationsphase* (ISBN: 978-3-425-73642-6). Die *Skills pages* geben dir Hilfestellungen zu wichtigen Aufgabenformaten. In den *Workshops* werden bestimmte Kompetenzen intensiv trainiert. Im Schulbuch werden außerdem weitere Aspekte der Themen dieses Arbeitsheftes behandelt.

The Story of an Hour – A short story (1894)

1

First read the information about the characters from the short story. Try to predict what their roles in the plot of the story might be.

- Louise Mallard: married to Brently Mallard, suffering from a heart disease

_____

_____

- Brently Mallard: husband to Louise Mallard, supposedly involved in a train accident

_____

_____

- Josephine: Louise's sister, worried about her

_____

_____

- Richards: Brently's friend, coming with some ominous information

_____

_____

The Story of an Hour

by Kate Chopin

Knowing that Mrs. Mallard was afflicted with a heart trouble, great care was taken to break to her as gently as possible the news of her husband's death.

It was her sister Josephine who told her, in broken
5 sentences; veiled[1] hints that revealed in half concealing. Her husband's friend Richards was there, too, near her. It was he who had been in the newspaper office when intelligence[2] of the railroad disaster was received, with Brently Mallard's name leading the list of "killed." He had
10 only taken the time to assure himself of its truth by a second telegram, and had hastened to forestall[3] any less careful, less tender friend in bearing the sad message.

She did not hear the story as many women have heard the same, with a paralyzed inability to accept its significance.
15 She wept at once, with sudden, wild abandonment, in her sister's arms. When the storm of grief had spent itself she went away to her room alone. She would have no one follow her.

There stood, facing the open window, a comfortable,
20 roomy armchair. Into this she sank, pressed down by a physical exhaustion[4] that haunted[5] her body and seemed to reach into her soul.

She could see in the open square before her house the tops of trees that were all aquiver[6] with the new spring
25 life. The delicious breath of rain was in the air. In the

Annotations
[1] **veiled** = disguised, concealed
[2] **intelligence** = information, news
[3] to **forestall** = to anticipate sth and prevent it from happening
[4] **exhaustion** = the state of being extremely tired and having no energy left
[5] to **haunt** = to appear repeatedly, to cause repeated anxiety or suffering
[6] **aquiver** = shaking or trembling, often because of strong emotion

street below a peddler[7] was crying his wares[8]. The notes of a distant song which some one was singing reached her faintly, and countless sparrows[9] were twittering in the eaves.

There were patches of blue sky showing here and there through the clouds that had met and piled one above the other in the west facing her window.

She sat with her head thrown back upon the cushion of the chair, quite motionless, except when a sob came up into her throat and shook her, as a child who has cried itself to sleep continues to sob in its dreams.

She was young, with a fair, calm face, whose lines bespoke[10] repression and even a certain strength. But now there was a dull stare in her eyes, whose gaze was fixed away off yonder[11] on one of those patches of blue sky. It was not a glance of reflection, but rather indicated a suspension of intelligent thought.

There was something coming to her and she was waiting for it, fearfully. What was it? She did not know; it was too subtle and elusive[12] to name. But she felt it, creeping out of the sky, reaching toward her through the sounds, the scents[13], the color that filled the air.

Now her bosom[14] rose and fell tumultuously[15]. She was beginning to recognize this thing that was approaching to possess her, and she was striving to beat it back with her will – as powerless as her two white slender[16] hands would have been.

When she abandoned herself a little whispered word escaped her slightly parted lips. She said it over and over under her breath: "free, free, free!" The vacant[17] stare and the look of terror that had followed it went from her eyes. They stayed keen and bright. Her pulses beat fast, and the coursing blood warmed and relaxed every inch of her body.

She did not stop to ask if it were or were not a monstrous joy that held her. A clear and exalted[18] perception enabled her to dismiss the suggestion as trivial.

She knew that she would weep again when she saw the kind, tender hands folded in death; the face that had never looked save with love upon her, fixed and gray and dead. But she saw beyond that bitter moment a long procession of years to come that would belong to her

absolutely. And she opened and spread her arms out to them in welcome.

There would be no one to live for her during those coming years; she would live for herself. There would be no powerful will bending hers in that blind persistence with which men and women believe they have a right to impose[19] a private will upon a fellow-creature. A kind intention or a cruel intention made the act seem no less a crime as she looked upon it in that brief moment of illumination[20].

And yet she had loved him – sometimes. Often she had not. What did it matter! What could love, the unsolved mystery, count for in face of this possession of self-assertion[21] which she suddenly recognized as the strongest impulse of her being!

"Free! Body and soul free!" she kept whispering.

Josephine was kneeling before the closed door with her lips to the keyhole, imploring[22] for admission. "Louise, open the door! I beg; open the door – you will make yourself ill. What are you doing, Louise? For heaven's sake open the door."

"Go away. I am not making myself ill." No; she was drinking in a very elixir[23] of life through that open window.

Her fancy was running riot along those days ahead of her. Spring days, and summer days, and all sorts of days that would be her own. She breathed a quick prayer that life might be long. It was only yesterday she had thought with a shudder that life might be long.

She arose at length and opened the door to her sister's importunities[24]. There was a feverish triumph in her eyes, and she carried herself unwittingly like a goddess of Victory. She clasped her sister's waist, and together they descended the stairs. Richards stood waiting for them at the bottom.

Some one was opening the front door with a latchkey[25]. It was Brently Mallard who entered, a little travel-stained[26], composedly carrying his grip-sack[27] and umbrella. He had been far from the scene of accident, and did not even know there had been one. He stood amazed at Josephine's piercing cry[28]; at Richards' quick motion to screen him from the view of his wife.

But Richards was too late.

When the doctors came they said she had died of heart disease – of joy that kills.

---

[7] **peddler** = a person who sells small goods, usually in the street or by going from door to door
[8] **ware** = goods
[9] **sparrow** = *Spatz*
[10] to **bespeak** = to show, to indicate
[11] **yonder** = over there
[12] **elusive** = difficult to describe, hard to grasp
[13] **scent** = a pleasant natural smell
[14] **bosom** = a person's chest
[15] **tumultuous** = highly agitated, confused or disturbed
[16] **slender** = thin and graceful
[17] **vacant** = empty, blank
[18] **exalted** = sublime, powerful

[19] to **impose** sth **on** sb = to force sth on sb
[20] **illumination** = spiritual enlightenment
[21] **self-assertion** = insistence on your own opinions, needs and wishes
[22] to **implore** = to beg
[23] **elixir** = a liquid with magical powers to preserve or improve sth
[24] **importunity** = persistence in demanding sth in a forceful and annoying way
[25] **latchkey** = a key for an outer door or gate
[26] **travel-stained** = dirty as a result of travelling
[27] **gripsack** (AE) = travel bag
[28] **piercing cry** = a loud, high-pitched and very sharp sound

WHILE READING

2

Read the short story. Match the sentence parts. Write the letters A–F in the boxes.

1	Richards …	☐	A	has a heart disease.
2	After hearing about Brently's death,	☐	B	Louise dies from a heart attack.
3	Louise …	☐	C	Louise witnesses Brently coming home.
4	Even though she loved him, …	☐	D	tells Louise that her husband has been killed in an accident.
5	Heading back downstairs, …	☐	E	Brently's death means a new sense of freedom for Louise.
6	Being shocked at the sight of Brently, …	☐	F	Louise reacts with immediate grief.

3

Short stories often follow a certain scheme. Look at the main elements and features of typical short stories. Then fill in the grid for "The Story of an Hour".

A typical short story		"The Story of an Hour"
1	… has an exposition or quickly throws the reader into the story without a lot of explanations.	
2	… has a theme.	
3	… focuses on one or two protagonists.	
4	… may have further characters.	
5	… has a single or limited setting.	
6	… is less complex and has a limited plot.	
7	… mostly includes a conflict.	
8	… doesn't contain a lot of development.	
9	… has a climax.	
10	… has an open ending.	
11	… has a limited number of words.	
12	… isn't divided into chapters.	
13	… doesn't show a lot of development of the characters. However, the story depicts an important moment in the characters' lives.	
14	… needs to be read more than once so that the reader can delve deeper into it and read between the lines. (Give examples.)	

POST-READING

4 **Group work**

Discuss: What is the main idea of "The Story of an Hour"?

5

Analyse the setting of the story: Why is it essential to the story? Could the story have taken place somewhere else?

6 **Group work**

What does the final phrase "joy that kills" (l. 111) mean? Explain.

7

The 'heart' appears to be a central symbol in the short story. Analyse in which contexts it is used in the story and what it could stand for.

8

The short story was originally published under the title "The Dream of an Hour".
Speculate why it has been changed to "The Story of an Hour".

9 **CHOOSE**

Creative writing: Brently's reaction to his wife's death is not shown in Kate Chopin's short story.
Continue the story by adding information about Brently experiencing the incident.
OR
Create a comic strip: Retell the story in five cartoon sketches with captions or speech/thought bubbles.
Focus on the following scenes:
• Richards coming to tell Louise about her husband's death
• Louise's first reaction to the news
• going up to her room and her second reaction to the news
• Josephine getting Louise back downstairs
• Brently walking in and Louise having a heart attack

Weekend – A short story (1978)

PRE-READING

1

What are your first associations	W
with the word 'weekend'?	E
Write an acrostic poem by	E
using the letters as initials or	K
placing them in the middle of a	E
word or sentence.	N
	D

— **Info** —

Acrostic

An acrostic is a poem in which particular letters, for example the first letters of each line, make a new word or phrase.

2

What do you expect a short story titled "Weekend" to deal with?
Note down your ideas.

_____

_____

_____

Weekend

by Fay Weldon

By seven-thirty they were ready to go. Martha had everything packed into the car and the three children appropriately dressed and in the back seat, complete with educational games and wholewheat[1] biscuits. When
5 everything was ready in the car Martin would switch off the television, come downstairs, lock up the house, front and back, and take the wheel.

Weekend! Only two hours' drive down to the cottage on Friday evenings: three hours' drive back on Sunday
10 nights. The pleasures of greenery[2] and guests in between. They reckoned themselves fortunate, how fortunate!

On Fridays Martha would get home on the bus at six-twelve and prepare tea and sandwiches for the family: then she would strip four beds and put the sheets and
15 quilt covers in the washing machine for Monday: take the country bedding from the airing basket, plus the books and the games, plus the weekend food – acquired[3] at intervals throughout the week, to lessen the load – plus her own folder of work from the office, plus
20 Martin's drawing materials (she was a market researcher in an advertising agency, he a freelance[4] designer) plus hairbrushes, jeans, spare T-shirts, Jolyon's antibiotics (he suffered from sore throats), Jenny's recorder, Jasper's cassette player and so on – ah, the so on! – and would
25 pack them all, skilfully and quickly, into the boot. Very little could be left in the cottage during the week. ('An open invitation to burglars[5]': Martin) Then Martha would run round the house tidying and wiping, doing this and that, finding the cat at one neighbour's and
30 delivering it to another, while the others ate their tea; and would usually, proudly, have everything finished by the time they had eaten their fill. Martin would just catch the BBC2 news, while Martha cleared away the tea table, and the children tossed[6] up for the best positions in the
35 car. 'Martha,' said Martin, tonight, 'you ought to get Mrs Hodder to do more. She takes advantage of you.'

Mrs Hodder came in twice a week to clean. She was over seventy. She charged two pounds an hour. Martha paid her out of her own wages: well, the running of the house
40 was Martha's concern. If Martha chose to go out to work

– as was her perfect right, Martin allowed, even though it wasn't the best thing for the children, but that must be Martha's moral responsibility – Martha must surely pay her domestic stand-in. An evident truth, heard loud and
45 clear and frequent in Martin's mouth and Martha's heart. 'I expect you're right,' said Martha. She did not want to argue. Martin had had a long hard week, and now had to drive. Martha couldn't. Martha's licence had been suspended[7] four months back for drunken driving.
50 Everyone agreed that the suspension was unfair; Martha seldom drank to excess: she was for one thing usually too busy pouring drinks for other people or washing other people's glasses to get much inside herself. But Martin had taken her out to dinner on her birthday, as was his
55 custom, and exhaustion[8] and excitement mixed had made her imprudent[9], and before she knew where she was, why there she was, in the dock[10], with a distorted lamp-post to pay for and a new bonnet[11] for the car and six months' suspension.

60 So now Martin had to drive her car down to the cottage, and he was always tired on Fridays, and hot and sleepy on Sundays, and every rattle[12] and clank[13] and bump in the engine she felt to be somehow her fault.

Martin had a little sports car for London and work: it
65 could nip in and out of the traffic nicely: Martha's was an old estate car, with room for the children, picnic baskets, bedding, food, games, plants, drink, portable television and all the things required by the middle classes for weekends in the country. It lumbered[14] rather than zipped
70 and made Martin angry. He seldom spoke a harsh word, but Martha, after the fashion of wives, could detect his mood from what he did not say rather than what he did, and from the tilt[15] of his head, and the way his crinkly[16], merry eyes seemed crinklier and merrier still – and of
75 course from the way he addressed Martha's car.

'Come along, you old banger[17] you! Can't you do better than that? You're too old, that's your trouble. Stop complaining. Always complaining, it's only a hill. You're too wide about the hips. You'll never get through there.'

Annotations

[1] **wholewheat** = made from flour that contains all the natural features of the wheat grain
[2] **greenery** = green plants, vegetation
[3] to **acquire** = to get, buy or obtain
[4] **freelance** = self-employed, doing pieces of work for different organizations
[5] **burglar** = a thief who enters a building to steal things
[6] to **toss up** = to gamble or to throw a coin in the air in order to make a decision between two alternatives
[7] **suspended** = stopped from being active; *here:* not allowed to drive as a form of punishment for drunken driving
[8] **exhaustion** = a state of extreme tiredness
[9] **imprudent** = thoughtless, not considering the consequences
[10] **in the dock** = in court
[11] **bonnet** = the metal cover over a car engine
[12] **rattle** = a series of short, sharp knocking sounds
[13] **clank** = a sharp, metallic sound
[14] to **lumber** = to move slowly and clumsily
[15] **tilt** = a sloping position
[16] **crinkly** = full of small lines and folds
[17] **banger** = *(infml.)* an old car in very bad condition

80 Martha worried about her age, her tendency to complain, and the width of her hips. She took the remarks personally. Was she right to do so? The children noticed nothing: it was just funny lively laughing Daddy being witty about Mummy's car. Mummy, done for drunken driving.

85 Mummy, with the roots of melancholy somewhere deep beneath the bustling, busy, everyday self. Busy: ah so busy!

Martin would only laugh if she said anything about the way he spoke to her car and warn her against paranoia.

90 'Don't get like your mother, darling.' Martha's mother had, towards the end, thought that people were plotting against her. Martha's mother had led a secluded[18], suspicious life, and made Martha's childhood a chilly and a lonely time. Life now, by comparison, was wonderful

95 for Martha. People, children, houses, conversations, food, drink, theatres – even, now, a career. Martin standing between her and the hostility[19] of the world – popular, easy, funny Martin, beckoning the rest of the world into earshot[20].

100 Ah, she was grateful: little earnest Martha, with her shy ways and her penchant[21] for passing boring exams – how her life had blossomed out! Three children too – Jasper, Jenny and Jolyon – all with Martin's broad brow and open looks, and the confidence born of her love and care,

105 and the work she had put into them since the dawning[22] of their days.

Martin drives. Martha, for once, drowses[23].

The right food, the right words, the right play. Doctors for the tonsils[24]: dentists for the molars[25]. Confiscate guns:

110 censor television: encourage creativity. Paints and paper to hand: books on the shelves: meetings with teachers. Music teachers. Dancing lessons. Parties. Friends to tea. School plays. Open days. Junior orchestra.

Martha is jolted awake[26]. Traffic lights. Martin doesn't

115 like Martha to sleep while he drives.

Clothes. Oh, clothes! Can't wear this: must wear that. Dress shops. Piles of clothes in corners: duly[27] washed, but waiting to be ironed, waiting to be put away.

Get the piles off the floor, into the laundry baskets.

120 Martin doesn't like a mess.

Creativity arises out of order, not chaos. Five years off work while the children were small: back to work with

seniority[28] lost. What, did you think something was

125 for nothing? If you have children, mother, that is your reward. It lies not in the world.

Have you taken enough food? Always hard to judge.

Food. Oh, food! Shop in the lunch-hour. Lug[29] it all home. Cook for the freezer on Wednesday evenings while Martin is at his car-maintenance[30] evening class, and isn't

130 there to notice you being unrestful. Martin likes you to sit down in the evenings. Fruit, meat, vegetables, flour for home-made bread. Well, shop bread is full of pollutants[31]. Frozen food, even your own, loses flavour. Martin often remarks on it. Condiments[32]. Everyone loves mango

135 chutney. But the expense!

London Airport to the left. Look, look, children! Concorde? No, idiot, of course it isn't Concorde.

Ah, to be all things to all people: children, husband, employer, friends! It can be done: yes, it can: super

140 woman.

Drink. Home-made wine. Why not? Elderberries[33] grown thick and rich in London: and at least you know what's in it. Store it in high cupboards: lots of room: up and down the step-ladder. Careful! Don't slip. Don't break anything.

145 No such thing as an accident. Accidents are Freudian slips[34]: they are wilful, bad-tempered things.

Martin can't bear bad temper. Martin likes slim ladies. Diet. Martin rather likes his secretary. Diet. Martin admires slim legs and big bosoms[35]. How to achieve them

150 both? Impossible. But try, oh try, to be what you ought to be, not what you are. Inside and out.

Martin brings back flowers and chocolates: whisks[36] Martha off for holiday weekends. Wonderful! The best husband in the world: look into his crinkly, merry,

155 gentle eyes; see it there. So the mouth slopes away into something of a pout[37]. Never mind. Gaze into the eyes. Love. It must be love. You married him. *You.* Surely *you* deserve true love?

Salisbury Plain[38]. Stonehenge[39]. Look, children, look!

160 Mother, we've seen Stonehenge a hundred times. Go back to sleep.

Cook! Ah cook. People love to come to Martin and Martha's dinners. Work it out in your head in the lunch-

---

[18] **secluded** = quiet, private and quite isolated
[19] **hostility** = unfriendly or aggressive behaviour
[20] **earshot** = the distance within which a sound or voice can be heard
[21] **penchant** = a special liking for sth
[22] **dawning** = daybreak; beginning
[23] to **drowse** = to be almost asleep or to sleep lightly
[24] **tonsil** = one of two small organs situated on each side of the throat at the back of the mouth
[25] **molar** = a large tooth at the back of the mouth
[26] to **jolt** sb **awake** = to wake sb up suddenly and violently
[27] **duly** = properly, as expected

[28] **seniority** = a higher rank and privileged position earned at work
[29] to **lug** = (infml.) to carry or drag sth with effort (because it is heavy)
[30] **car maintenance** = the activity of checking a vehicle regularly and, when necessary, repairing it
[31] **pollutant** = a harmful substance
[32] **condiment** = any spice or sauce that is added to food to improve its taste
[33] **elderberry** = *Holunderbeere*
[34] **Freudian slip** = accidentally saying sth that reveals your hidden thoughts
[35] **bosom** = a woman's breasts
[36] to **whisk** = to take sb or sth somewhere else quickly
[37] **pout** = a position of the lips that shows displeasure or annoyance
[38] **Salisbury Plain** = a large area of flat land north of Salisbury in southern England
[39] **Stonehenge** = a circle of very large stones, a famous prehistoric monument in southern England

hour. If you get in at six-twelve, you can seal the meat while you beat the egg white while you feed the cat while you lay the table while you string the beans while you set out the cheese, goat's cheese, Martin loves goat's cheese, Martha tries to like goat's cheese – oh, bed, sleep, peace, quiet.

Sex! Ah sex. Orgasm, please. Martin requires it. Well, so do you. And you don't want his secretary providing a passion you neglected[40] to develop. Do you? Quick, quick, the cosmic bond. Love. Married love.

Secretary! Probably a vulgar suspicion: nothing more.

Probably a fit of paranoics, à la mother, now dead and gone.

At peace.

RIP.

Chilly, lonely mother, following her suspicions where they led.

Nearly there, children. Nearly in paradise, nearly at the cottage. Have another biscuit.

Real roses round the door.

Roses. Prune[41], weed[42], spray, feed, pick. Avoid thorns.

One of Martin's few harsh words.

'Martha, you can't not want roses! What kind of person am I married to? An anti-rose personality?'

Green grass. Oh, God, grass. Grass must be mowed. Restful lawns, daisies bobbing[43], buttercups glowing.

Roses and grass and books. Books.

Please, Martin, do we have to have the two hundred books, mostly twenties' first editions, bought at Christie's book sale on one of your afternoons off? Books need dusting.

Roars of laughter from Martin, Jasper, Jenny and Jolyon.

Mummy says we shouldn't have the books: books need dusting!

Roses, green grass, books and peace.

Martha woke up with a start when they got to the cottage, and gave a little shriek which made them all laugh. Mummy's waking shriek, they called it.

Then there was the car to unpack and the beds to make up, and the electricity to connect, and the supper to make, and the cobwebs[44] to remove, while Martin made the fire. Then supper – pork chops in sweet and sour sauce ('Pork is such a *dull* meat if you don't cook it properly': Martin), green salad from the garden, or such green salad as the rabbits had left ('Martha, did you really net them properly? Be honest now!': Martin) and sauté[45] potatoes.

Mash is so stodgy[46] and ordinary, and instant mash unthinkable. The children studied the night sky with the aid of their star map. Wonderful, rewarding children!

Then clear up the supper: set the dough to prove for the bread: Martin already in bed: exhausted by the drive and lighting the fire. ('Martha, we really ought to get the logs[47] stacked properly. Get the children to do it, will you?': Martin) Sweep and tidy: get the TV aerial[48] right. Turn up Jasper's jeans where he has trodden the hem[49] undone. ('He can't go around like *that*, Martha. Not even Jasper': Martin)

Midnight. Good night. Weekend guests arriving in the morning. Seven for lunch and dinner on Saturday. Seven for Sunday breakfast, nine for Sunday lunch. ('Don't fuss[50], darling. You always make such a fuss': Martin) Oh, God, forgotten the garlic squeezer. That means ten minutes with the back of a spoon and salt. Well, who wants *lumps* of garlic? No one. Not Martin's guests. Martin said so. Sleep.

Colin and Katie. Colin is Martin's oldest friend. Katie is his new young wife. Janet, Colin's other, earlier wife, was Martha's friend.

Janet was rather like Martha, quieter and duller than her husband. A nag[51] and a drag[52], Martin rather thought, and said, and of course she'd let herself go, everyone agreed. No one exactly excused Colin for walking out, but you could see the temptation.

Katie versus Janet.

Katie was languid[53], beautiful and elegant. She drawled when she spoke. Her hands were expressive: her feet were little and female. She had no children.

Janet plodded[54] round on very flat, rather large feet. There was something wrong with them. They turned out slightly when she walked. She had two children. She was, frankly, boring. But Martha liked her: when Janet came down to the cottage she would wash up. Not in the way that most guests washed up – washing dutifully and setting everything out on the draining board[55], but actually drying and putting away too. And Janet would wash the bath and get the children all sat down, with chairs for everyone, even the littlest, and keep them quiet and satisfied so the grown-ups – well, the men – could get on with their conversation and their jokes and their

Annotations

[40] to **neglect** = to fail to give enough care or attention to sb or sth

[41] to **prune** = to cut off parts from a plant to make it grow better

[42] to **weed** = to remove wild (unwanted) plants from a place in a garden or field

[43] to **bob** = to move up and down

[44] **cobweb** = a net made by a spider

[45] **sauté** = fried quickly in a little oil or fat

[46] **stodgy** = heavy and difficult to digest

[47] **log** = a piece of wood cut for burning on a fire

[48] **aerial** = a piece of metal wire that can receive or send out radio or television signals

[49] **hem** = the edge of a piece of cloth that is folded over and sewn

[50] to **fuss** = to give too much attention to unimportant matters

[51] **nag** = a person who is always complaining or criticizing

[52] **drag** = *(infml.)* a person who is unpleasant and boring

[53] **languid** = showing little energy or interest (often in an attractive way)

[54] to **plod** = to walk slowly and heavily

[55] **draining board** = the place next to a sink where the dishes are left to dry after they have been washed

love of country weekends, while Janet stared into space, as if grateful for the rest, quite happy.

Janet would garden, too. Weed the strawberries, while the
255 men went for their walk; her great feet standing firm and square and sometime crushing a plant or so, but never mind, oh never mind. Lovely Janet; who understood.

Now Janet was gone and here was Katie.

Katie talked with the men and went for walks with the
260 men, and moved her ashtray rather impatiently when Martha tried to clear the drinks round it.

Dishes were boring, Katie implied[56] by her manner, and domesticity[57] was boring, and anyone who bothered with that kind of thing was a fool. Like Martha. Ash should be
265 allowed to stay where it was, even if it was in the butter, and conversations should never be interrupted.

Knock, knock. Katie and Colin arrived at one-fifteen on Saturday morning, just after Martha had got to bed. 'You don't mind? It was the moonlight. We couldn't resist
270 it. You should have seen Stonehenge! We didn't disturb you? Such early birds!'

Martha rustled up a quick meal of omelettes. Saturday nights' eggs. ('Martha makes a lovely omelette': Martin) ('Honey, make one of your mushroom omelettes: cook
275 the mushrooms separately, remember, with lemon. Otherwise the water from the mushrooms gets into the egg, and spoils everything.') Sunday supper mushrooms. But ungracious[58] to say anything.

Martin had revived wonderfully at the sight of Colin and
280 Katie. He brought out the whisky bottle. Glasses. Ice. Jug[59] for water. Wait. Wash up another sinkful, when they're finished. 2 a.m.

'Don't do it tonight, darling.'

'It'll only take a sec.' Bright smile, not a hint of self-
285 pity[60]. Self-pity can spoil everyone's weekend.

Martha knows that if breakfast for seven is to be manageable the sink must be cleared of dishes. A tricky meal, breakfast. Especially if bacon, eggs, and tomatoes must all be cooked in separate pans. ('Separate pans
290 mean separate flavours!': Martin)

She is running around in her nightie[61]. Now if that had been Katie – but there's something so *practical* about Martha. Reassuring, mind; but the skimpy[62] nightie and the broad rump[63] and the thirty-eight years are all rather
295 embarrassing. Martha can see it in Colin and Katie's eyes. Martin's too. Martha wishes she did not see so much

in other people's eyes. Her mother did, too. Dear, dead mother. Did I misjudge[64] you?

This was the second weekend Katie had been down with
300 Colin but without Janet. Colin was a photographer: Katie had been his accessorizer. First Colin and Janet: then Colin, Janet and Katie: now Colin and Katie!

Katie weeded with rubber gloves on and pulled out pansies[65] in mistake for weeds and laughed and laughed
305 along with everyone when her mistake was pointed out to her, but the pansies died. Well, Colin had become with the years fairly rich and fairly famous, and what does a fairly rich and famous man want with a wife like Janet when Katie is at hand?

310 On the first of the Colin/Janet/Katie weekends Katie had appeared out of the bathroom. 'I say,' said Katie, holding out a damp[66] towel with evident distaste, 'I can only find this. No hope of a dry one?' And Martha had run to fetch a dry towel and amazingly found one, and handed
315 it to Katie who flashed her a brilliant smile and said, 'I can't bear damp towels. Anything in the world but damp towels,' as if speaking to a servant in a time of shortage of staff, and took all the water so there was none left for Martha to wash up.

320 The trouble, of course, was drying anything at all in the cottage. There were no facilities for doing so, and Martin had a horror of clothes lines which might spoil the view. He toiled and moiled[67] all week in the city simply to get a country view at the weekend. Ridiculous to spoil it by
325 draping it with wet towels! But now Martha had bought more towels, so perhaps everyone could be satisfied. She would take nine damp towels back on Sunday evenings in a plastic bag and see to them in London.

On this Saturday morning, straight after breakfast,
330 Katie went out to the car – she and Colin had a new Lamborghini; hard to imagine Katie in anything duller – and came back waving a new Yves St Laurent towel. 'See! I brought my own, darlings.'

They'd brought nothing else. No fruit, no meat, no
335 vegetables, not even bread, certainly not a box of chocolates. They'd gone off to bed with alacrity[68], the night before, and the spare room rocked and heaved: well, who'd want to do washing-up when you could do that, but what about the children? Would they get confused?
340 First Colin and Janet, now Colin and Katie?

Martha murmured something of her thoughts to Martin, who looked quite shocked. 'Colin's my best friend. I don't expect him to bring anything,' and Martha felt mean.

---

56 to **imply** = to express sth indirectly
57 **domesticity** = life at home, family life
58 **ungracious** = rude, impolite
59 **jug** = a container for liquids
60 **self-pity** = a feeling of unhappiness or sadness for yourself
61 **nightie** *(infml.)* = nightdress
62 **skimpy** = not large enough, made of too little material
63 **rump** = a person's bottom

64 to **misjudge** = to form an unfair opinion or a wrong idea about sb or sth
65 **pansy** = *Stiefmütterchen (Pflanze)*
66 **damp** = slightly wet
67 to **toil and moil** = to work hard
68 **with alacrity** = quickly and eagerly

13

'And good heavens, you can't protect the kids from sex for ever: don't be so prudish[69],' so that Martha felt stupid as well. Mean, complaining, and stupid.

Janet had rung Martha during the week. The house had been sold over her head, and she and the children had been moved into a small flat. Katie was trying to persuade Colin to cut down on her allowance[70], Janet said.

'It does one no good to be materialistic,' Katie confided. 'I have nothing. No home, no family, no ties, no possessions. Look at me! Only me and a suitcase of clothes.' But Katie seemed highly satisfied with the me, and the clothes were stupendous. Katie drank a great deal and became funny. Everyone laughed, including Martha. Katie had been married twice. Martha marvelled at how someone could arrive in their mid-thirties with nothing at all to their name, neither husband, nor children, nor property and not mind.

Mind you, Martha could see the power of such helplessness. If Colin was all Katie had in the world, how could Colin abandon her? And to what? Where would she go? How would she live? Oh, clever Katie.

'My teacup's dirty,' said Katie, and Martha ran to clean it, apologizing, and Martin raised his eyebrows, at Martha, not Katie.

'I wish *you'd* wear scent[71],' said Martin to Martha, reproachfully[72]. Katie wore lots. Martha never seemed to have time to put any on, though Martin bought her bottle after bottle. Martha leapt out of bed each morning to meet some emergency – miaowing cat, coughing child, faulty alarm clock, postman's knock – when was Martha to put on scent? It annoyed Martin all the same. She ought to do more to charm him.

Colin looked handsome and harrowed[73] and younger than Martin, though they were much the same age. 'Youth's catching,' said Martin in bed that night. 'It's since he found Katie.' Found, like some treasure. Discovered; something exciting and wonderful, in the dreary[74] world of established spouses[75].

On Saturday morning Jasper trod on a piece of wood ('Martha, why isn't he wearing shoes? It's too bad': Martin) and Martha took him into the hospital to have a nasty splinter removed. She left the cottage at ten and arrived back at one, and they were still sitting in the sun, drinking, empty bottles glinting in the long grass. The grass hadn't been cut. Don't forget the bottles. Broken glass means more mornings at the hospital. Oh, don't fuss. Enjoy yourself. Like other people. Try.

But no potatoes peeled, no breakfast cleared, nothing. Cigarette ends still amongst old toast, bacon rind[76] and marmalade. 'You could have done the potatoes,' Martha burst out. Oh, bad temper! Prime sin. They looked at her in amazement and dislike. Martin too.

'Goodness,' said Katie. 'Are we doing the whole Sunday lunch bit on Saturday? Potatoes? Ages since I've eaten potatoes. Wonderful!'

'The children expect it,' said Martha.

So they did. Saturday and Sunday lunch shone like reassuring beacons[77] in their lives. Saturday lunch: family lunch: fish and chips. ('So much better cooked at home than bought': Martin) Sunday. Usually roast beef, potatoes, peas, apple pie. Oh, of course. Yorkshire pudding. Always a problem with oven temperatures. When the beef's going slowly, the Yorkshire should be going fast. How to achieve that? Like big bosom and little hips.

'Just relax,' said Martin. 'I'll cook dinner, all in good time. Splinters always work their own way out: no need to have taken him to hospital. Let life drift over you, my love. Flow with the waves, that's the way.'

And Martin flashed Martha a distant, spiritual smile. His hand lay on Katie's slim brown arm, with its many gold bands.

'Anyway, you do too much for the children,' said Martin. 'It isn't good for them. Have a drink.'

So Martha perched[78] uneasily on the step and had a glass of cider, and wondered how, if lunch was going to be late, she would get cleared up and the meat out of the marinade for the rather formal dinner that would be expected that evening. The marinaded lamb ought to cook for at least four hours in a low oven; and the cottage oven was very small, and you couldn't use that and the grill at the same time and Martin liked his fish grilled, not fried. Less cholesterol[79].

She didn't say as much. Domestic details like this were very boring, and any mild complaint was registered by Martin as a scene. And to make a scene was so ungrateful. This was the life. Well, wasn't it? Smart friends in large cars and country living and drinks before lunch and roses and bird song – 'Don't drink *too* much,' said Martin, and told them about Martha's suspended driving licence.

The children were hungry so Martha opened them a can of beans and sausages and heated that up. ('Martha, do they have to eat that crap? Can't they wait?': Martin)

Annotations

[69] **prudish** = easily shocked by rude things or anything relating to sex
[70] **allowance** = money that is given to sb on a regular basis, financial support
[71] **scent** = perfume
[72] **reproachful** = expressing criticism
[73] **harrowed** = looking as if you have suffered
[74] **dreary** = boring, dull and depressing
[75] **spouse** = husband or wife

[76] **bacon rind** = the outer edge of a slice of bacon
[77] **beacon** = a light or fire that acts as a signal
[78] to **perch** = to sit down on the edge of sth
[79] **cholesterol** = *Cholesterin*

Katie was hungry: she said so, to keep the children in face. She was lovely with children – most children. She did not particularly like Colin and Janet's children. She said so, and he accepted it. He only saw them once a month now, not once a week.

'Let me make lunch,' Katie said to Martha. 'You do so much, poor thing!'

And she pulled out of the fridge all the things Martha had put away for the next day's picnic lunch party – Camembert cheese and salad and salami and made a wonderful tomato salad in two minutes and opened the white wine – 'not very cold, darling. Shouldn't it be chilling?' – and had it all on the table in five amazing competent minutes. 'That's all we need, darling,' said Martin. 'You are funny with your fish-and-chip Saturdays! What could be nicer than this? Or simpler?'

Nothing, except there was Sunday's buffet lunch for nine gone, in place of Saturday's fish for six, and would the fish stretch? No. Katie had had quite a lot to drink. She pecked[80] Martha on the forehead. 'Funny little Martha,' she said. 'She reminds me of Janet. I really do like Janet.' Colin did not want to be reminded of Janet, and said so. 'Darling, Janet's a fact of life,' said Katie. 'If you'd only think about her more, you might manage to pay her less.' And she yawned and stretched her lean[81], childless body and smiled at Colin with her inviting, naughty little girl eyes, and Martin watched her in admiration.

Martha got up and left them and took a paint pot and put a coat of white gloss on the bathroom wall. The white surface pleased her. She was good at painting. She produced a smooth, even surface. Her legs throbbed[82]. She feared she might be getting varicose veins[83].

Outside in the garden the children played badminton. They were bad-tempered, but relieved to be able to look up and see their mother working, as usual: making their lives for ever better and nicer: organizing, planning, thinking ahead, side-stepping disaster, making preparations, like a mother hen, fussing and irritating: part of the natural boring scenery of the world.

On Saturday night Katie went to bed early: she rose from her chair and stretched and yawned and poked her head into the kitchen where Martha was washing saucepans. Colin had cleared the table and Katie had folded the napkins into pretty creases[84], while Martin blew at the fire, to make it bright. 'Good night,' said Katie.

Katie appeared three minutes later, reproachfully holding out her Yves St Laurent towel, sopping wet. 'Oh dear,' cried Martha. 'Jenny must have washed her hair!' And Martha was obliged to rout[85] Jenny out of bed to rebuke[86] her, publicly, if only to demonstrate that she knew what was right and proper. That meant Jenny would sulk[87] all weekend, and that meant a treat or an outing mid-week, or else by the following week she'd be having an asthma attack. 'You fuss the children too much,' said Martin. 'That's why Jenny has asthma.' Jenny was pleasant enough to look at, but not stunning. Perhaps she was a disappointment to her father? Martin would never say so, but Martha feared he thought so.

An egg and an orange each child, each day. Then nothing too bad would go wrong. And it hadn't. The asthma was very mild. A calm, tranquil environment, the doctor said. Ah, smile, Martha smile. Domestic happiness depends on you. 21 x 52 oranges a year. Each one to be purchased, carried, peeled and washed up after. And what about potatoes. 12 x 52 pounds a year? Martin liked his potatoes carefully peeled. He couldn't bear to find little cores of black in the mouthful. ('Well, it isn't very nice, is it?': Martin).

Martha dreamt she was eating coal, by handfuls, and liking it.

Saturday night. Martin made love to Martha three times. Three times? How virile[88] he was, and clearly turned on by the sounds from the spare room. Martin said he loved her. Martin always did. He was a courteous[89] lover; he knew the importance of foreplay. So did Martha. Three times.

Ah, sleep. Jolyon had a nightmare. Jenny was woken by a moth[90]. Martin slept through everything. Martha pottered[91] about the house in the night. There was a moon. She sat at the window and stared out into the summer night for five minutes, and was at peace, and then went back to bed because she ought to be fresh for the morning.

But she wasn't. She slept late. The others went out for a walk. They'd left a note, a considerate note: 'Didn't wake you. You looked tired. Had a cold breakfast so as not to make too much mess. Leave everything 'til we get back.' But it was ten o'clock, and guests were coming at noon, so she cleared away the bread, the butter, the crumbs, the smears[92], the jam, the spoons, the spilt sugar, the cereal, the milk (sour by now) and the dirty plates, and swept

[80] to **peck** = *here:* to give sb a quick, light kiss
[81] **lean** = thin and in good physical condition
[82] to **throb** = to pulsate
[83] **varicose veins** = a condition in which the veins, especially in the legs, are swollen and can be seen on the skin
[84] **crease** = a line on cloth or paper where it has been folded

[85] to **rout** sb **out** = to force or drive out
[86] to **rebuke** = to speak severely or angrily to sb because they have said or done sth that you think is wrong
[87] to **sulk** = to be silent and bad-tempered because you are angry about sth
[88] **virile** = masculine, full of strength and sexual energy
[89] **courteous** = polite and respectful
[90] **moth** = an insect which usually flies at night and is attracted to light
[91] to **potter about/around** (BE) = to move around or do unimportant things without hurrying, in a pleasant way
[92] **smear** = a dirty mark

the floors, and tidied up quickly, and grabbed a cup of coffee, and prepared to make a rice and fish dish, and a
530 chocolate mousse and sat down in the middle to eat a lot of bread and jam herself. Broad hips. She remembered the office work in her file and knew she wouldn't be able to do it. Martin anyway thought it was ridiculous for her to bring work back at the weekends. 'It's your holiday,' he'd
535 say. 'Why should they impose[93]?' Martha loved her work. She didn't have to smile at it. She just did it.

Katie came back upset and crying. She sat in the kitchen while Martha worked and drank glass after glass of gin and bitter lemon. Katie liked ice and lemon in gin. Martha
540 paid for all the drink out of her wages. It was part of the deal between her and Martin – the contract by which she went out to work. All things to cheer the spirit, otherwise depressed by a working wife and mother, were to be paid for by Martha. Drink, holidays, petrol, outings, puddings,
545 electricity, heating: it was quite a joke between them. It didn't really make any difference: it was their joint[94] money, after all. Amazing how Martha's wages were creeping up, almost to the level of Martin's. One day they would overtake. Then what?
550 Work, honestly, was a piece of cake[95].

Anyway, poor Katie was crying. Colin, she'd discovered, kept a photograph of Janet and the children in his wallet. 'He's not free of her. He pretends he is, but he isn't. She has him by a stranglehold[96]. It's the kids. His bloody kids.
555 Moaning Mary and that little creep Joanna. It's all he thinks about. I'm nobody.'

But Katie didn't believe it. She knew she was somebody all right. Colin came in, in a fury. He took out the photograph and set fire to it, bitterly, with a match. Up in
560 smoke they went. Mary and Joanna and Janet. The ashes fell on the floor. (Martha swept them up when Colin and Katie had gone. It hardly seemed polite to do so when they were still there.) 'Go back to her,' Katie said. 'Go back to her. I don't care. Honestly, I'd rather be on my
565 own. You're a nice old fashioned thing. Run along then. Do your thing, I'll do mine. Who cares?'

'Christ, Katie, the fuss! She only just happens to be in the photograph. She's not there on purpose to annoy. And I do feel bad about her. She's been having a hard
570 time.'

'And haven't you, Colin? She twists a pretty knife, I can tell you. Don't you have rights too? Not to mention me. Is a little loyalty too much to expect?'

They were reconciled[97] before lunch, up in the spare room.
575 Harry and Beryl Elder arrived at twelve-thirty. Harry didn't like to hurry on Sundays; Beryl was flustered with apologies for their lateness. They'd brought artichokes from their garden. 'Wonderful,' cried Martin. 'Fruits of the earth? Let's have a wonderful soup! Don't fret[98],
580 Martha. I'll do it.'

'Don't fret.' Martha clearly hadn't been smiling enough. She was in danger, Martin implied, of ruining everyone's weekend. There was an emergency in the garden very shortly – an elm[99] tree which had probably got Dutch
585 elm disease – and Martha finished the artichokes. The lid flew off the blender and there was artichoke purée everywhere. 'Let's have lunch outside,' said Colin. 'Less work for Martha.'

Martin frowned at Martha: he thought the appearance of
590 martyrdom[100] in the face of guests to be an unforgivable offence.

Everyone happily joined in taking the furniture out, but it was Martha's experience that nobody ever helped to bring it in again.
595 Jolyon was stung by a wasp. Jasper sneezed and sneezed from hay fever[101] and couldn't find the tissues and he wouldn't use loo[102] paper. ('Surely you remembered the tissues, darling?': Martin)

Beryl Elder was nice. 'Wonderful to eat out,' she said,
600 fetching the cream for her pudding, while Martha fished a fly from the liquefying[103] Brie[104] ('You shouldn't have bought it so ripe, Martha': Martin) – 'except it's just some other woman has to do it. But at least it isn't *me*.' Beryl worked too, as a secretary, to send the boys to boarding
605 school, where she'd rather they weren't. But her husband was from a rather grand family, and she'd been only a typist when he married her, so her life was a mass of amends[105], one way or another. Harry had lately opted out of the stockbroking[106] rat race and become an artist,
610 choosing integrity rather than money, but that choice was his alone and couldn't of course be inflicted on the boys. Katie found the fish and rice dish rather strange, toyed[107] at it with her fork, and talked about Italian restaurants she knew. Martin lay back soaking in the sun: crying,
615 'Oh, this is the life.' He made coffee, nobly, and the lid

flew off the grinder[108] and there were coffee beans all over the kitchen especially in amongst the row of cookery books which Martin gave Martha Christmas by Christmas. At least they didn't have to be brought back 620 every weekend. ('The burglars won't have the sense to steal those': Martin)

Beryl fell asleep and Katie watched her, quizzically[109]. Beryl's mouth was open and she had a lot of fillings, and her ankles were thick and her waist was going, and she 625 didn't look after herself. 'I love women,' sighed Katie. 'They look so wonderful asleep. I wish I could be an earth mother.' Beryl woke with a start and nagged her husband into going home, which he clearly didn't want to do, so didn't. Beryl thought she had to get back because his mother was 630 coming round later. Nonsense! Then Beryl tried to stop Harry drinking more home-made wine and was laughed

at by everyone. He was driving, Beryl couldn't, and he did have a nasty scar on his temple from a previous road accident. Never mind.

635 'She does come on strong, poor soul,' laughed Katie when they'd finally gone. 'I'm never going to get married,' – and Colin looked at her yearningly[110] because he wanted to marry her more than anything in the world, and Martha cleared the coffee cups.

640 'Oh don't *do* that,' said Katie, 'do just sit *down*, Martha, you make us all feel bad,' and Martin glared at Martha who sat down and Jenny called out for her and Martha went upstairs and Jenny had started her first period and Martha cried and cried and knew she must stop because 645 this must be a joyous occasion for Jenny or her whole future would be blighted[111], but for once, Martha couldn't. Her daughter Jenny: wife, mother, friend.

---

[108] **grinder** = a kitchen device for crushing food into small pieces or a powder
[109] **quizzically** = in a way that seems to ask a question

[110] **yearningly** = in a way that expresses a strong desire for sth
[111] **blighted** = spoiled, ruined

WHILE READING

 3

Read the short story and answer the following questions.

a) Where are Martha, Martin and their children heading for the weekend?

_____

_____

b) What do they carry with them to their destination?

_____

_____

c) Who turns up unexpectedly for the weekend?

_____

_____

d) What is Martha's reaction to the surprise visit? What is Martin's?

_____

_____

e) Who is Janet?

_____

_____

f) What happens on Saturday?

_____

_____

g) More visitors turn up for Sunday lunch. Who are they?

_____

_____

4

Choose the best adjectives to describe Martha's relationship with Martin. Explain your choice in class.

> affectionate | dependent | intimate | strong | disdaining | special | selfish | traditional | fussy | difficult | close | supportive | submissive | inferior | committed | devoted

5

Reread the short story. Pay special attention to Martin's comments which are inserted in brackets. Speculate what they might suggest.

6

Explain why Martha cries at the end of the story.

POST-READING

7 Group work (3)

Read the short story again. Work in a group of three. Each of you chooses one of the following characters: Martha, Martin or Katie.

a) Use the grid below to note down what you have learned about them and provide evidence from the text.

b) Present your results to the other members of your group and add the missing information.

	Martha	Martin	Katie
Outer appearance (e.g. physical features, clothes, body language)			
Behaviour (how the character acts)			

	Martha	Martin	Katie
Mood (the emotional state of the character)			
Relationship to other people (how the character interacts with others and is perceived by them)			
Evidence from the text			

c) Write a coherent characterization of one of the characters using appropriate quotations from the short story.
→ **Workshop:** Analysing characters   → **S12:** Checklist: Analysis – prose   → **S23:** How to quote

Language support

Writing a characterization

The protagonist is described/depicted as ... | He/She seems to be ... | He/She appears to be ... |
He/She likes to be ... | He/She is portrayed as ... | His/Her behaviour clearly indicates that ... |
The fact that he/she ... reveals/proves that ... | It is quite apparent that ...

8
Compare Martha and Katie.

9   CHOOSE

Pair work Imagine a conversation in the car as Martha and Martin drive back to London. What will Martin say about the weekend? What is Martha's response? Write and act out their conversation.
OR
The story is told from Martha's point of view. Describe what happened at the weekend from Martin's point of view.

10 Pair work

Create a freeze-frame portraying Martha's and Martin's relationship.

11

Do you think there are typical jobs around the house that should be done by women/men? Why (not)? Form a double circle and discuss.

The First Feminists – A short story (2020)

PRE-READING

1

Look at the picture and think of a caption.

Info

Feminism

Feminism is a social, political and economic movement based on the belief that women all over the world should have equal social, economic and political rights and freedoms. It stresses and advocates the equality of the sexes. No person should be denied certain rights – such as the right to vote – because of their sex and gender. Yet, feminism goes beyond basic rights and seeks deeper cultural shifts like rethinking gender norms, sexism and self-expression. Since the late 18th century, there have been public campaigns for women's rights fighting for educational, professional and interpersonal improvement for women. Among feminism's successes are important personal rights such as owning property and receiving education. However, these rights are not guaranteed in every country of the world. This is also true for legal access to contraception and legal abortion, or protection from domestic violence. Feminism is manifested worldwide and keeps on fighting against societal obstacles preventing women from equal rights and treatment.

2

After having looked at the picture and having read the information in the box, outline your expectations of the short story "The First Feminists".

_____

_____

_____

_____

The First Feminists

by Bernardine Evaristo

we were there when you were just becoming human, unaware that we were carrying the futures of countless billions of souls in our yet to be discovered DNA, unaware we would go on reproducing ever-evolving[1] versions
5 of ourselves, that as the reason for the foetus in every mother's womb[2], we were the Founding Mothers[3] of the Human Gene Pool

of that we are so proud, we say, when we get together for our annual Founding Mother's Reunion, it dominates
10 the conversation – the human race is here because of us, we boast, only to ourselves, sadly, because nobody can see us, which is a shame, what with the obsession with ancestry DNA these days, we'd love to present ourselves to the world, in the flesh – sashaying[4] down the runway
15 of time in our glad rags[5], as weird and wonderful role models from pre-history

we were there when you were just becoming human, although we didn't know it back then, we didn't know that humans were beginning to evolve into existence, after the
20 planet's land mass had floated apart and reformed into continents, after the world had gone into a deep freeze during the ice ages, and ice sheets covered the earth and sea, after mountainous[6] icebergs rose up into the cold, blue landscape, sucking the water of the seas into
25 their peaks and freezing them, draining the waterways, which became hollow basins, exposing the continental shelves[7] hidden several miles below in the underground world of oceans, after the ice melted, and the world re-emerged, and the glacial plains[8] of the Sahara thawed[9]
30 out and burst forth with the green and glorious colours of tropical vegetation and impenetrable[10] rainforest, and became ripe with all the fruits and teeming[11] with all the wildlife

we were the first tribes, the first clans, we were the original
35 trailblazers[12], after enough of us had developed a maternal instinct towards our offspring[13], after we stopped walking away from the curious thing that had ejected itself from our bodies, after enough of us learned that the children born out of siblings copulating[14] with each other, and also
40 with their parents, would, in two or three generations, be born with a terrible weakness passed on for generations to come, after we learned to trek[15] and hunt in search of food, and discovered there was more land to be found out there in The Great Unknown, after we became intelligent
45 enough to create fire, a powerful, artificial heat, and to work with bone and stone, after our brains expanded, our arms shortened, our legs lengthened until finally we became fully upright and slowly made progress with The Great Migration of Humankind, and eventually arrived
50 at a location near you – Asia, America, Australasia[16], the Arctic, Europe, and all over Africa, our homeland, where we all began

it was tough in the early years, we like to remind each other at our decennial[17] Founding Mother's Reunion,
55 we love indulging[18] in 21st Century social customs like pretending to drink tea and eating biscuits, playacting[19] at being contemporary humans, when we've actually been around for mega-annums[20], in one form or another, and how we laughed at the millennium celebrations just
60 the other day, marking the transition from the 20th to the 21st Century, as if it was such a big deal, our descendants really haven't lived at all, unlike us

we who risked extinction[21] over and over again from lack of food or water, from too much heat or too much
65 cold, we who risked extinction from the relentless[22] battles, especially when our food sources dried up, or when others came onto the territory we'd claimed as ours, and when our tribal squabbles[23] led to internecine

Annotations

1 **ever-evolving** = developing continuously
2 **womb** = the organ inside the body of a woman (or female mammal) in which a baby grows before it is born
3 **founding mother/father** = a person who establishes an important institution, movement or idea
4 to **sashay** = to walk gracefully and confidently, in a way that attracts attention
5 **glad rags** *(infml.)* = best clothes or clothes for special occasions
6 **mountainous** = having or relating to mountains; very large, huge
7 **continental shelf** = the edge of a continent that lies under the ocean
8 **glacial plains** = a flat mass of sand, mud and other material deposited by a moving or melting glacier
9 to **thaw out** = to get warm gradually after being very cold
10 **impenetrable** = impossible to enter or get through
11 to **teem with** = to be full of

12 **trailblazer** = pioneer, the first person to do sth
13 **offspring** = a person's children or the young of an animal
14 to **copulate** = to have sexual intercourse
15 to **trek** = to walk a long way over land
16 **Australasia** = the region of Australia, New Zealand and neighbouring islands in the Pacific Ocean
17 **decennial** = occurring every ten years
18 to **indulge in** = to allow oneself to enjoy the pleasure of sth
19 to **playact** = to make believe
20 **mega-annum** = a period of 1 million years
21 **extinction** = the death of all living members of a species
22 **relentless** = harsh and persistent
23 **squabble** = a noisy quarrel over an unimportant matter

warfare[24] about who was boss, once we discovered the
power of power, once we realised that having it meant a
better chance of survival, and being in control could be
intoxicating

we women were all alpha females back in the day, we had
to be to survive, we were so formidable, we'd have it out
with anyone who gave us grief, whether male or female,
and believe us when we say, you didn't mess with the
Founding Mothers, the First Ladies of Humanity, because
we gave as good as we got, we fought back like the beasts
we all were, we women didn't run screaming when we
were confronted with human foes and expect men to
defend us, we often attacked first, it was in us, we had
the primal energy to do combat[25], we owned our physical
strength

the concepts of femininity and masculinity did not
exist back in the day, the idea of women behaving in a
"'ladylike'" fashion took ages to become normalised, we
first humans of Planet Earth shat where we were, farted
and burped with impunity, modesty was a future concept,
we sexed whenever we felt like it, wore no clothes, not
even animal skins or tree barks, not at first, and when we
menstruated, we left a trail of blood

we women were equal to men, it was only mothering
that tethered[26] our ambitions, when it became our sole
responsibility because men liked power so much they
wanted to keep it all for themselves, but before then,
childrearing[27] was shared equally between all of us,
shared between our clan, until the males among us began
to pack more muscle density and grow taller, and began
to assume the upper hand, demanding we stay with the
children rather than go hunting for dinner, for our family,
for our clan

we women fought back, we never stopped fighting
back, sometimes we won and men were forced to live
in a matriarchal[28] society, other times men won and we
lived in a patriarchy, sometimes neither dominated and
we were egalitarian[29], which was ideal, we were the first
communists, but it never lasted long because the human

desire to dominate each other prevailed[30], among us were
the first control freaks, dictators, emotional manipulators,
domestic abusers – and we women survived it all, we
women survived everything pre-civilisation had to throw
at us, we were the ultimate survival experts, we survived
on nuts and berries, in the early days of human life, could
go days without water, we slept rough, lived dangerously,
fought wild animals, protected our young

luckily for the human race, dinosaurs died out 64 million
years before we emerged, we could not have co-existed
on the same planet, our small communities roaming[31] the
plains on two legs would have ended up as their hors
d'oeuvres[32], eaten live, eaten raw

we were the world's first female leaders, the first
feminists, the badass bitches of evolution, whose names
will never be remembered because we had no names,
we were anonymous, we will never be recognised as
individuals for our incredible global achievements in
ensuring the continuation of the human race, although
we lived long before egos became part of being human,
we do want to be remembered for what we achieved,
and we are saddened that we have been reduced to
a few fossils and the imaginations of archaeologists
who haven't really got a clue about our lives, how we
lived, the different ways in which we died – death by
disease, before herbs, incantations[33], health and safety
regulations, and medicine, and death by murder, death
by tribal warfare, and death by religious sacrifice, once
we started to worship deities[34] – animate and inanimate,
seen and unseen, once we became intelligent enough to
want to make sense of the world we lived in and imagined
supreme, all knowing beings who could help us in times
of crisis

for the longest time we mated without love, we did not
know the meaning of it, although in time we evolved to
have feelings for each other, the modern-day concept
of love still amuses us, all the songs sung about it when
companionship and compatibility[35] are more important,
we all agree on that, love is a feeling but if the human
race is to survive then we all have to get along

Annotations

[24] **internecine warfare** = destructive fighting which takes place between opposing groups in a country or organization

[25] **combat** = a fight or a battle

[26] **to tether** = to tie sth (especially an animal) with a rope or chain to restrict its movement

[27] **childrearing** = the process of bringing up children

[28] **matriarchal** = controlled by women

[29] **egalitarian** = believing that all people are equal and should have the same rights and opportunities

[30] **to prevail** = to predominate

[31] **to roam** = to move around without a particular purpose

[32] **hors d'oeuvre** = a small dish that is usually served as an appetizer before the main part of a meal

[33] **incantation** = a series of words said or sung as a magic spell

[34] **deity** = a god or goddess

[35] **compatibility** = the ability to exist or work together successfully with sth or sb else

it might seem odd telling you all this now when it was eons[36] ago, but our lives were important to us and we have been so overlooked, so misunderstood, and we are the only ones who know it, sometimes at our Founding Mothers Reunion, after we've had a few gin and tonics and feel relaxed and comforted by our company, we all fall silent and return to our pre-language selves, to a time when we humans were hyper-sensitive to each other, when we sensed more than we thought, when that was enough, when our first sounds were inarticulate grunts, it took an age for words to come into being and many hundreds of thousands of years for us to create language, to join the words up into sentences, and many more for writing to be invented

imagine a world where there are no words to describe your fellow human beings, no words for animals, to describe the trees, the forest, the sea, a child, imagine a world where there was no word for the concept of family, now we know all the words in all the languages, thousands of them, we have so much knowledge stored in our infinite memory banks, we are knowledge and because we take the long view, we worry about what the future holds, we look up into the exploding stars from a society we never imagined and wonder aloud – what will the human race become? how will we evolve?

we discuss our fears that the human race will annihilate[37] itself before too long, dehydrate the planet so that it once more dies of thirst, all plant and animal life withered[38] in the heat, we worry that cannibalism will return, which is what happens when starving people have to resort to desperate measures, we worry about the appearance of new diseases that science cannot control, we worry that humans will detonate[39] themselves into inexistence with the last great wars of this civilisation, perhaps there'll be a global Armageddon[40] of megalomaniacal[41]

warlords[42] who are capable of human eradication[43], of planetary destruction, we worry that hackers encoded encryptions[44] will one day collapse the cybers-structures without which this society cannot function – the internet virus that finally closed the world down – the civilisation you are looking for is no longer available

we worry that everything we fought for might one day no longer be here, except for us, hovering in the air, a ghostly presence neither seen, heard or felt by modern human beings who have lost their extra sensory perception, and we will feel so sad that our endeavours over millions of years might one day come to an end, and then we decide to cheer ourselves up by wallowing in nostalgia, because we are happiest in the past, when we were younger, more truly alive and everything was new

we remember a time before the internet, before computers, before laws
before cars, aeroplanes, bicycles, penny farthings[45] and horse-drawn carriages
before factories, before politics, before royalty, before money, before houses
before agriculture, before the idea of work, before marriage, before enslavement
before the formation of countries, governments, before leisure and social lives
before cooked food, before sophisticated cognitive reasoning, before science
before pollution, before manufacture, education, dancing, poetry
before we could plan ahead, could think outside of ourselves
before we were able to tell our own stories
before our songs were sung
we were there
we were there
we were there

[36] **eon** = an indefinitely long period of time
[37] to **annihilate** = to destroy completely
[38] **withered** = dry and decaying, losing vitality
[39] to **detonate** = to explode or to cause sth to explode
[40] **Armageddon** = a catastrophic and extremely destructive conflict; the end of the world
[41] **megalomaniacal** = having a very strong desire for power

[42] **warlord** = a military leader who controls an area
[43] **eradication** = complete destruction
[44] **encryption** = the process of converting information into a secret code
[45] **penny farthing** = a type of bicycle with a very large front wheel and a small back wheel which was used in the past

WHILE READING

3

Read the short story.

a) Divide the story into meaningful parts.

b) Give every part a heading.

c) Summarize the story.

4

Explain the following quote:

"we worry that everything we fought for might one day no longer be here, except for us [...]" (ll. 189–190)

5

Describe the role of women as depicted in the short story. Do men play any role?

POST-READING

6

a) **Think:** Make a list of three themes you consider central to your understanding of the short story.

b) **Pair:** Explain your choices to a partner and agree on three major themes.

c) **Share:** Discuss your results in a small group and agree on three themes, giving reasons for your choice by presenting examples from the short story.

7

Bernardine Evaristo hardly uses any punctuation in her short story.

a) Rewrite the short story using punctuation.

b) How do you decide where to put a comma, question mark or full stop?

c) How does it change the understanding and meaning of the text if more punctuation is used?

d) Discuss in class why Bernardine Evaristo might have decided to leave out most of the punctuation.

Post-reading: The short stories

1

Compare the short stories you have read. What similarities are there and what differences can you identify?

Similarities	Differences

2

Look at the quotes taken from the short stories. Choose the one you like best or consider most relevant. Explain the context of the quote and analyse its relevance for the short story.

> And yet she had loved him – sometimes. Often she had not. What did it matter! What could love, the unsolved mystery, count for in face of this possession of self-assertion which she suddenly recognized as the strongest impulse of her being!
> *("The Story of an Hour")*

> She didn't say as much. Domestic details like this were very boring, and any mild complaint was registered by Martin as a scene. And to make a scene was so ungrateful.
> *("Weekend")*

> [...] before then, childrearing was shared equally between all of us, shared between our clan, until the males among us began to pack more muscle density and grow taller, and began to assume the upper hand, [...]
> *("The First Feminists")*

> There would be no powerful will bending hers in that blind persistence with which men and women believe they have a right to impose a private will upon a fellow-creature.
> *("The Story of an Hour")*

> we women fought back, we never stopped fighting back, sometimes we won and men were forced to live in a matriarchal society, other times men won and we lived in a patriarchy, sometimes neither dominated and we were egalitarian, [...]
> *("The First Feminists")*

> If Martha chose to go out to work – as was her perfect right, Martin allowed, even though it wasn't the best thing for the children, but that must be Martha's moral responsibility – Martha must surely pay her domestic stand-in.
> *("Weekend")*

Notes:

_____

_____

_____

_____

_____

_____

_____

3

Discuss in class what the quotes tell us about female roles and gender equality.

The individual and society

QUESTIONS OF IDENTITY – AMBITIONS AND OBSTACLES

1   Pair work

Look at the diagram and the photos below. What do they tell you in terms of people's ambitions and obstacles in society? Discuss with a partner.

Half or more say being poor, Muslim, black or Hispanic puts people at a disadvantage in our society

% saying being each of the following helps/hurts people's ability to get ahead in our country these days

■ Hurts a lot   ■ Hurts a little   ■ Helps a little   ■ Helps a lot

Being ...	Hurts a lot	Hurts a little	Helps a little	Helps a lot	Neither helps nor hurts
White	4	7	21	38	28
Asian	3	18	26	8	44
Native American	16	22	16	7	37
Hispanic	17	35	11	6	30
Black	25	30	10	7	26
Evangelical Christian	5	10	19	11	54
Jewish	4	16	15	8	55
Muslim	31	32	5	3	27
A man	3	7	28	38	24
A woman	10	41	15	8	25
Wealthy	2	2	11	78	7
Poor	66	20	3	2	8

Note: Share of respondents who didn't offer an answer not shown.
Source: Survey of U.S. adults conducted Jan. 22-Feb. 5, 2019
"Race in America 2019"

PEW RESEARCH CENTER

Language support

The survey shows ... / Photo number ... shows ...

There are a lot of obstacles concerning ...

It hurts a little/a lot to be ...

In contrast to ...

If you compare people's ambitions and obstacles in society, one can say ...

1

2

3

4

2 Pair work

Describe and analyse the infographic below.

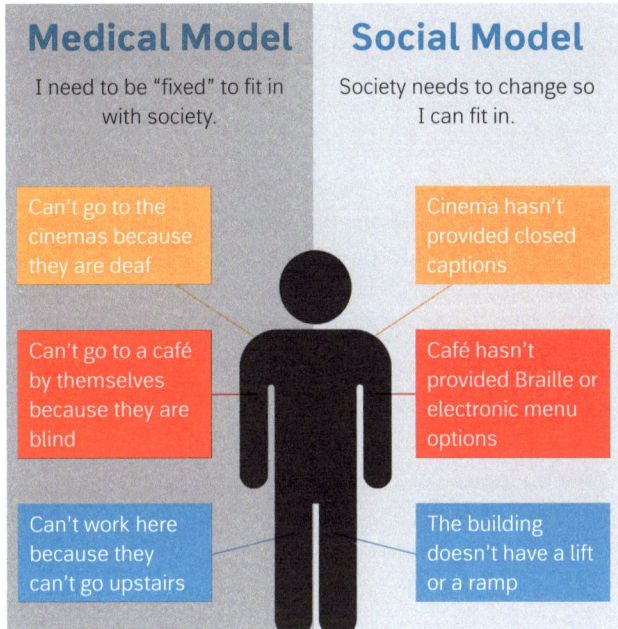

3 Pair work

a) List obstacles that people with disabilities face in their work life.

b) Find solutions to the obstacles listed in a).

4

Milling around: Talk to at least five classmates about your ambitions and goals in life. Find out whether your classmates give the same or similar answers to your own.

5

a) Do some research on the term "from rags to riches".

b) Write a short entry on "from rags to riches" for an online dictionary.

c) Group work Discuss: Do you think that a "from rags to riches" story is still possible? If so, find famous persons as examples.

QUESTIONS OF IDENTITY – CONFORMITY VS. INDIVIDUALISM

6 → **Workshop:** Analysing a cartoon → **S17:** How to work with cartoons

a) Look at the cartoon and describe it.

b) Analyse its message.

c) Comment on the message of the cartoon.

"What's wrong with you?"

7

Read the following extract from an online article.

The Dangers of Conformity

By Paul Sloane   24/07/2023

Conformity can be defined as the act of following social norms, rules, or expectations in order to fit in or be accepted by a group.

While conformity can be beneficial in some situ-
5 ations, such as following traffic rules to ensure safety, there are also dangers associated with conformity, including:

- Loss of individuality: Conformity can lead to a loss of individuality as people may suppress
10 their own opinions and ideas in order to fit in with a group. This can result in a lack of creativity and innovation, as well as a failure to address important issues.

- Groupthink: Conformity can lead to groupthink,
15 which is a situation where a group of people makes decisions based on maintaining group harmony rather than objective analysis of the situation. This can lead to poor decision-making and can be particularly dangerous in situations
20 where the stakes are high, such as in politics or business.

- Discrimination and prejudice: Conformity can lead to discrimination and prejudice as people may conform to the beliefs and attitudes of a
25 group, even if those beliefs and attitudes are discriminatory or prejudiced.

- Inhibition of personal growth: Conformity can inhibit personal growth as people may avoid taking risks or pursuing their own goals in
30 order to conform to societal norms or group expectations.

- Failure to question authority: Conformity can result in a failure to question authority, which can lead to acceptance of unjust or unethical
35 practices.

[...]

a) **Pair work** Write down four questions about the text to test your partner's knowledge.
b) Answer each other's questions.
c) Find at least one example for each danger of conformity described in the article.
d) Discuss in class: What are the dangers of individualism? Can you think of any?

CHANCES AND CHALLENGES FOR SOCIETY – GENDER ISSUES

8

Look at the word cloud. What challenges for today's society can you spot?

9

a) What other challenges for society can you think of?

b) **Group work** Compare your results in your group.

c) Share your results in class and discuss which of the challenges can also be seen as chances for our future.

10

a) Describe the picture.

b) Look up unknown gender and orientation icons and create a legend for all of them.

11

What's the difference between 'gender' and 'sex'? Look up both terms and write a definition for each of them.

12

Comment on the following quote.

> "A gender-equal society would be one where the word 'gender' does not exist, where everyone can be themselves."
> – Gloria Steinem

13

You are going to listen to an extract from a *BBC* interview in which presenter Kim Chakanetsa talks to two women fighting for equality with men in their chosen sport. **Webcode** DSW-73699-01

First read the questions below. Then listen to the interview (up to 04:57) and answer the questions.

a) What is the big deal about equality for women's sports besides payment?

_____

b) What did Kathryn Bertine successfully lobby for?

_____

c) What makes Hajra Khan so special in her profession?

_____

d) What is money in terms of equality in women's sport according to Hajra Khan?

_____

e) What goes hand in hand according to Kathryn Bertine?

_____

f) Where did Hajra Khan use to train?

_____

g) How was the enormous pay gap between male and female football players justified?

_____

h) Until when were women in cycling denied a bigger salary?

_____

14 **Group work**

Have a formal debate on the following statement: "Female athletes deserve equal pay to men."
- Get into six groups and prepare the debate. Three groups collect arguments in favour of the statement, the other three groups collect arguments against it.
- Choose a chairperson to act as a 'referee'. He/She opens the debate and keeps track of the time (e.g. a one-minute time limit for each speaker).
- Each group chooses their first speaker (the others can join the discussion later). Start the debate through the chairperson.
- Take turns in arguing for or against the statement. The chairperson always introduces the next speaker.
- Open the debate for questions from the floor.
- In the end, the chairperson closes the debate.

Useful phrases for the chairperson:

- Ladies and gentlemen, today's motion is equal pay in sports. Team A is going to argue in favour of the motion, team B is going to argue against it. May the best team win! We'll start with a first person in favour of the motion. …
- The debate is now open to the floor. …
- There are some questions from the audience. …
- Now I would like to ask the audience to vote on the motion: Would those in favour of it please raise their hands? … Would those against the motion please raise their hands? … The motion is accepted/lost.

15 Pair work

What do you know about gender inequality? Talk to a partner.

16

Read five statements from *Human Rights Careers* on causes of gender inequality. What do you think? Match the given percentages and numbers to the statements below.

> 6 | 24.3% | 25% | 75% | 200

1. Around the world, women still have less access to education than men.

   _____ of young women between 15–24 will not finish primary school.

2. Only _____ countries in the world give women the same legal work rights as men.

3. In fact, most economies give women only _____ of the rights of men.

4. According to the World Health Organization, over _____ million women who don't want to get pregnant are not using contraception.

5. Of all national parliaments at the beginning of 2019, only _____ of seats were filled by women.

17 → **Workshop:** Mediation → **S19:** How to improve your mediation skills → **S7:** Checklist: Writing a blog post

Imagine you are an exchange student at a school in Britain. Your class is doing a project on gender roles around the world. You are asked to contribute a German perspective on the matter and found an opinion piece from *Deutschlandfunk Kultur*. Read the text below and use the information to write a blog post for the school website.

Gemeinsame Doppelnamen reichen nicht!

Ein Kommentar von Tanja Dückers • 03.04.2023

Soll es künftig beim Heiraten auch die Möglichkeit geben, die Nachnamen beider Partner zu verschmelzen? Dieser Vorschlag kam nicht in den aktuellen Entwurf des Justizministeriums.
5 *Autorin und Journalistin Tanja Dückers findet das falsch.*

Bundesjustizminister Marco Buschmann (FDP) will das Namensrecht reformieren und es Eheleuten ermöglichen, künftig gemeinsame Doppel-
10 namen zu führen. Auch die Grünen hatten eine Reform ins Gespräch gebracht: die Verschmelzung von Nachnamen.

Wie bei so manchen Vorschlägen der Grünen wurden sogleich in routiniert-reflexhafter Weise
15 hämische Stimmen laut. Doch bei näherer Betrachtung erscheint die Idee nicht so abwegig: Sie erlaubt Ehepartnern einen egalitären Kompromiss ohne endlose Doppelnamen oder den Verzicht auf einen der beiden Nachnamen.
20 Und doch wird eine Gemeinsamkeit betont, anders als bei dem Modell: Jeder behält den eigenen Namen, als wäre man nie miteinander in den Ehestand getreten.

Traditionelle Rollenbilder

25 In Ländern wie den USA oder Großbritannien ist dieses Meshing längst Praxis. Der ehemalige Bürgermeister von Los Angeles, Antonio Villaraigosa, hat seinen Nachnamen Villar mit dem seiner Frau Corina Raigosa verschmolzen. In vielen
30 spanischsprachigen Ländern haben die Bürger in der Regel zwei Nachnamen: einen vom Vater, einen von der Mutter.

Auch wenn der Vorschlag in Deutschland sicher nicht mit Breitenwirkung umgesetzt werden wird,
35 wirft er doch ein Licht auf ein wenig beachtetes Feld: Parität der Geschlechter herrscht in Deutschland bei der Annahme der Nachnamen nicht einmal entfernt.

Im Gegenteil: Allen bekannten Doppelnamen
40 zum Trotz kann man größtenteils immer noch die tradierte Rollenaufteilung beobachten. Bis 1991 war es geltendes Recht, dass der Ehemann den Ehenamen bestimmen darf. Inzwischen ist es über 30 Jahre her, seit dieses Gesetz gekippt wurde
45 und das Verfassungsgericht beschlossen hat, es sei unvereinbar mit dem Grundgesetz. Die angemahnte Reform trat drei Jahre später in Kraft: Seit 1994 können sich Ehepartnerinnen und -partner entscheiden, ihren Nachnamen zu
50 behalten.

Nur sechs Prozent wählen den Namen der Frau

Aber wie sieht die Realität aus? Nur jedes achte Ehepaar nutzt die Möglichkeit, den jeweils eigenen Nachnamen weiterhin zu behalten. Laut einer
55 Studie der Gesellschaft für deutsche Sprache von 2018 entscheidet sich ein Ehepaar in nur sechs Prozent der Fälle für den Nachnamen der Frau. Viel dürfte sich daran bisher nicht geändert haben. Dass sich nur so wenige Paare für den Namen der
60 Ehefrau entscheiden, liegt sicher nicht daran, dass Frauen die hässlicheren Nachnamen mit in die Ehe bringen. Männer argumentieren laut der genannten Studie häufig mit der Tradition. Sie empfänden es als Zeichen von Schwäche oder Unmännlichkeit,
65 den Namen der Frau anzunehmen. Frauen könnten jedoch ebenso argumentieren, etwa weil ein Name sonst in der Familienlinie aussterben würde oder weil er als wichtiger Teil der eigenen Identität begriffen wird.
70 Ein weiteres Argument für das Beibehalten des eigenen Namens laut Gesellschaft für deutsche Sprache: Wer schon Karriere gemacht hat, möchte seinen Namen nicht aufgeben. Bei Eheschließung sind Männer in Deutschland im Schnitt knapp drei
75 Jahre älter als Frauen. Somit wiegt ihr „Karriereargument" schwerer als das ihrer Partnerinnen.

Mauer, Hattmann und Schauck

Die Kritik selbst ernannter Sprachästheten kann man bei der Frage nach der Nachnamensregelung
80 getrost zurückweisen, wenn man sich einige der Doppelnamen-Wortungetüme von Personen des öffentlichen Lebens in Erinnerung ruft. Außerdem lässt sich über Geschmack bekanntlich nicht streiten. Es gibt Menschen, die ihre Kinder Rapunzel,
85 Waterloo oder Bierstübl nennen dürfen – diese Vornamen wurden in Deutschland tatsächlich erlaubt.

Dagegen klingen Mauer (Angela Merkel und Joachim Sauer), Hattmann (Marco Buschmann und
90 Janina Hatt) und Schauck (Joachim Gauck und Daniela Schadt, falls sie heiraten würden), doch vergleichsweise harmlos. Und Frau Leutheusser-Schnarrenberger könnte einfach Leutberger heißen – falls sie denn diesen Namen bevorzugen würde.

---

18 Group work

In our society, steps are being taken to improve gender equality and the equality of opportunities.
Prepare a card survey: Think about supportive measures that could be used to improve gender equality.
Note down your ideas on cards. Then present your ideas to the class and cluster the cards on the board.

19

Do some research on one of the following topics:
- violence against women
- empowerment of women
- balanced participation in decision-making
- gender mainstreaming
- gender stereotypes and sexism
- sex roles in contemporary western societies
- toys and games for boys and girls

Prepare a short presentation. You can also choose to record it as a podcast or to create a short video.

QUESTIONS OF IDENTITY AND GENDER ISSUES IN THE SHORT STORIES

Go back to the short stories you have read.

20

Name the different ambitions and obstacles the protagonists of the short stories have to deal with.

21

Provide as many examples of gender stereotypes and sexism from the short stories as you can.

22

Analyse the role of the institution of marriage in the short stories.

23   Pair work

Discuss which of the short stories present the most conformative character and the most individualized character. Give reasons for your choice.

24

Explain why all of the short stories can be considered feminist literature. Discuss your results in class.

25

Do you think it is important to read feminist literature at school? Why (not)?
Have a fishbowl discussion.

Info

Fishbowl discussion

A fishbowl discussion is an efficient way to practice group discussions.
Four to six students sit in a circle, the "fishbowl". Each of them first presents their arguments and then starts actively discussing the topic. The other students sit outside the "fishbowl" and listen carefully to their classmates' discussion.
There are two ways to organize a fishbowl discussion: a closed and an open "fishbowl".
In a closed "fishbowl", all chairs inside the "fishbowl" are occupied by students. The audience outside the circle listens and takes notes on who had the best arguments.
In an open "fishbowl", however, one or two chairs in the "fishbowl" remain empty and any member of the audience can, at any time, occupy an empty chair and join the discussion.
Students usually take turns in a fishbowl discussion to practice both discussing a topic and giving feedback to the contributors.

Pre-reading

1

You are going to read the novel *Behold the Dreamers* (2016) by Imbolo Mbue.

a) Examine the title and the book cover below.
   You can look at more book covers online:

   Webcode DSW-73699-02

   Try to paraphrase the title of the novel and assess the choice of words.

Info

According to *Oxford Languages*, the verb **behold** means "*(archaic, literary)* see or observe (someone or something, especially of remarkable or impressive nature)".
Example: "behold your lord and prince!"

Publisher: Random House
(Penguin Random House LLC), 2016

b) Based on your observations, speculate what the novel could be about.
   Make a mind map and note down your first ideas about the plot.

Behold the Dreamers

While reading

— Info —

A **reading map** will help you follow and keep track of the novel throughout the reading process, so you can review the plot easily and quickly, and access passages about characters, themes and motifs when working on specific topic tasks. Highlighting thoroughly saves you time and effort when analysing the novel.

2

While you read the novel, create your own reading guide through the narrative in the form of a reading map.

Use …

- **sticky notes** to summarize each chapter in as many sentences or bullet points as you need.
- **smaller strips** to mark passages in the book where important topics and motifs are mentioned.
- **different colours** to highlight crucial information about the characters, key words, sentences or passages.
- **symbols and abbreviations** to mark aspects such as topics and motifs which are weaved into the novel.

Examples:

☁	dream motif (a significant or recurrent theme)
☺ / ☹	themes of happiness/sadness
↔	dichotomies (for example, rich – poor, black – white, …)
$	information on somebody's job situation or financial background information
"…"	important quotes
!	crucial events
?!	indignation concerning an event or situation, surprise, or point for discussion
R / Cl–J	relationships (for example, between Clark and Jende)
pol / gov	issues that concern politics or the government
US	descriptions and perceptions of the United States

CHAPTER ONE

3

a) Describe the behaviour and feelings of Jende and Clark during their first encounter. Provide textual evidence and write the words and quotes around the characters below.

Adjectives to describe behaviour

condescending | respectful | submissive | nervous | insecure | rude | relieved | tense | busy | desperate | arrogant | demanding | undignified | disrespectful | benevolent | gracious | polite | welcoming | interested | ...

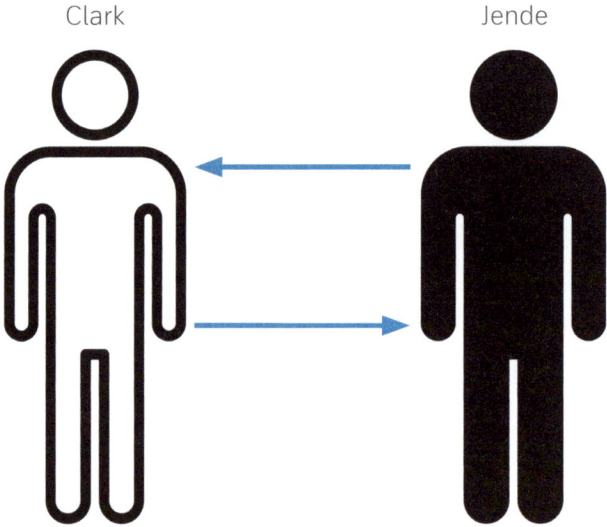

Clark   Jende

b) Assess Jende's and Clark's behaviour.

CHAPTERS TWO – THREE

4

Describe Neni's and Jende's dreams. Include quotes.

Neni   Jende

CHAPTERS FOUR – SIX

5

Create a (digital) web diagram about the family dynamics in the Edwards family.

6

Contrast Jende's descriptions of Limbe (Cameroon, Central Africa) and America.

Limbe:

_____

_____

_____

_____

_____

_____

_____

_____

_____

_____

_____

America:

_____

_____

_____

_____

_____

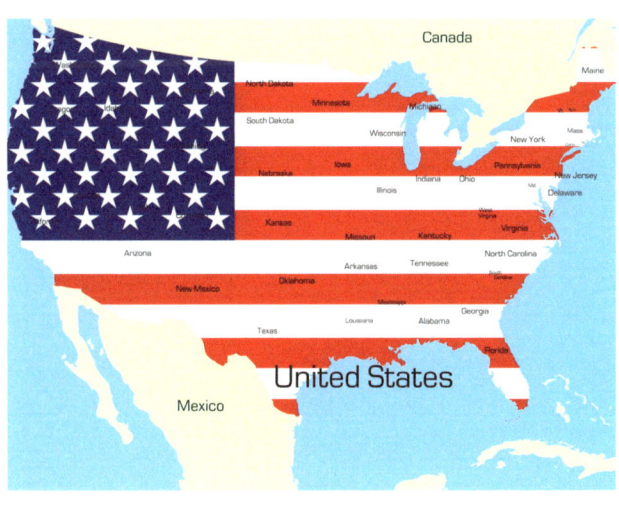

_____

_____

_____

CHAPTERS SEVEN – THIRTEEN

7

Summarize Leah's concerns about the Wall Street firm, Lehman Brothers.

8

Describe Neni's work ethic and the effect life in America has on her.

9

Explain the consequences of Jende's application for asylum not being approved.

10 **Pair work**

In order to recapitulate important issues and information in chapters 11 and 12, use the words in the boxes below and exchange information with your partner. You may also give opinions, add extra information, do some quick research, or raise questions. Be prepared to share your results in class.

Partner A: | truth and love | work permit | Obama | Hillary | police |

Partner B: | Professor | homosexuality | transgender | dishonesty | domestic violence |

11

a) Note down what you find out about Cindy's character in chapter 13.
b) Add what you find out from Cindy's phone conversation about Clark to your family dynamics web diagram from task 5.

CHAPTER FOURTEEN

12

Describe the situation in the bar and Neni's observations about 'belonging'.

13 → **S21:** How to succeed in oral exams

While waiting for Neni to come to the US, Jende "[…] often wondered if leaving home in search of something as fleeting as fortune was ever worthwhile." (p. 70)
Comment on his statement, using the think – pair – share method.

Info

Method: Think – pair – share

Think: What do you think? Make a list of pros and cons.
Pair: Based on your results, present your opinion and listen to your partner's.
Share: Discuss in a group of four.

✓ It is worth it because …	✗ It is not worth it because …

CHAPTERS FIFTEEN – SIXTEEN

14

a) Describe the difficulties that Lehman Brothers is facing.

b) Contrast Tom's stance with Clark's on how to deal with the issues at Lehman Brothers.

15 → **S9:** How to structure a text   → **S23:** How to quote

a) Analyse Vince's description of America.

b) Compare it to Jende's description in chapter 6.

CHAPTERS SEVENTEEN – TWENTY-FIVE

16 → **S12:** Checklist: Analysis – prose

a) Characterize Cindy Edwards.   → **Workshop:** Analysing characters

b) Analyse which concepts of 'home' are presented in these chapters.

CHAPTERS TWENTY-SIX – THIRTY-FOUR

17

a) Read the information about Lehman Brothers from the online encyclopedia *Britannica*.

b) Describe Jende's dream and the significant economic event.

c) List the consequences of the collapse.

d) Explain Jende's predicament concerning the Edwards family.

— Info —

Bankruptcy of Lehman Brothers, collapse of the investment bank Lehman Brothers that occurred on September 15, 2008. It was the largest bankruptcy in U.S. history at that time, and it was among the most significant events of the financial crisis of 2007–08. [...]

CHAPTERS THIRTY-FIVE – FORTY-THREE

18

Answer the following questions.

a) What important document does Jende receive?

_____

_____

b) What does Neni do to deal with the situation?

_____

_____

c) How does Jende perceive himself and his behaviour?

_____

_____

d) What does Clark need to see Jende about?

_____

_____

e) What are the effects of the new situation on Jende and Neni individually?

_____

_____

f) What are the effects on their relationship?

_____

_____

g) What does Neni do at the Edwards' home?

_____

_____

CHAPTERS FORTY-FOUR – FIFTY-FOUR

19 → **S12:** Checklist: Analysis – prose → **Workshop:** Analysing characters → **S8:** How to improve your text

a) Characterize Neni.

b) What is Neni considering doing in order to ensure that she and her family can stay in America? (Refer to chapters 44, 51 and 53.)

_____

_____

c) **Group work (3)** Work in groups of three. One of you is Neni, one of you tries to assert that her idea is beneficial, and one of you tries to convince her that it would be a fatal mistake. Write the dialogue and perform the role play.

d) Assess Neni's behaviour.

e) Neni says, "Maybe I'm becoming another person." (p. 229) Comment on her statement.

20

Decide whether the statements below are true or false. Provide evidence from the text for each statement.

	Statement	True	False	Evidence
1	Cindy Edwards dies due to the consumption of drugs in combination with alcohol.			
2	Neni feels guilty about Cindy's death because of her blackmail.			
3	The dean is very helpful and supports Neni's ambitions.			
4	Neni is grateful for the dean's realistic advice.			
5	Watching videos of the funeral after Pa Jonga's death makes up for the fact that Jende wasn't able to be there.			
6	Neni and Jende agree that they should leave the US.			
7	Before Neni arrived in the US, America was synonymous with happiness to her.			
8	Jende is remorseful after hitting Neni.			
9	Neni doesn't understand why Jende has turned into an abuser and can never forgive him.			
10	Jende applies for voluntary departure.			

21

a) Describe Jende's changed attitude towards America.
b) "I'm ready to go back home," (p. 212) Jende states. Explain what led to his decision.
c) Explain why Neni wants to stay in the US.

CHAPTERS FIFTY-FIVE – SIXTY-TWO

22

Describe the impact that Cindy's death has on Clark, Vince and Mighty.

23

Explain what Vince criticizes about American society.

24

Describe Jende's and Neni's thoughts concerning their future life in Cameroon and their present life in America after the request for voluntary departure has been granted.

25

Comment on this statement about Neni:
"[...] she was not one of them – she was now a woman of class [...]." (p. 261)

26

Analyse the meaning of the final question in the novel:

> "What did you say, Papa?" a drowsy and awakening Liomi asked.
> Jende turned from the front seat and looked at his son. "Guess where we are," he whispered.
> "Where?" Liomi asked, struggling to open his eyes.
> "Guess," Jende whispered again.
> The boy opened his eyes and said, "Home?" (p. 261)

Post-reading

27

Analyse how the relationship between Jende and Neni changes throughout the novel.

28

a) Examine what 'home' means to Jende and Clark.
b) Comment on the fact that the Jongas return to Limbe.

→ **Workshop:** Writing a comment → **S6:** How to write a discussion/comment

29 → **S12:** Checklist: Analysis – prose → **Workshop:** Analysing characters → **S8:** How to improve your text

Choose one of the following characters and write a characterization:

• Vince Edwards
• Jende Jonga
• Clark Edwards

30

a) Describe the relationship between Vince and his parents.
b) Examine the importance of family for Clark and Cindy Edwards.

31

A lot of things distinguish the Edwards family from the Jongas. Define the differences and then focus on what they have in common.

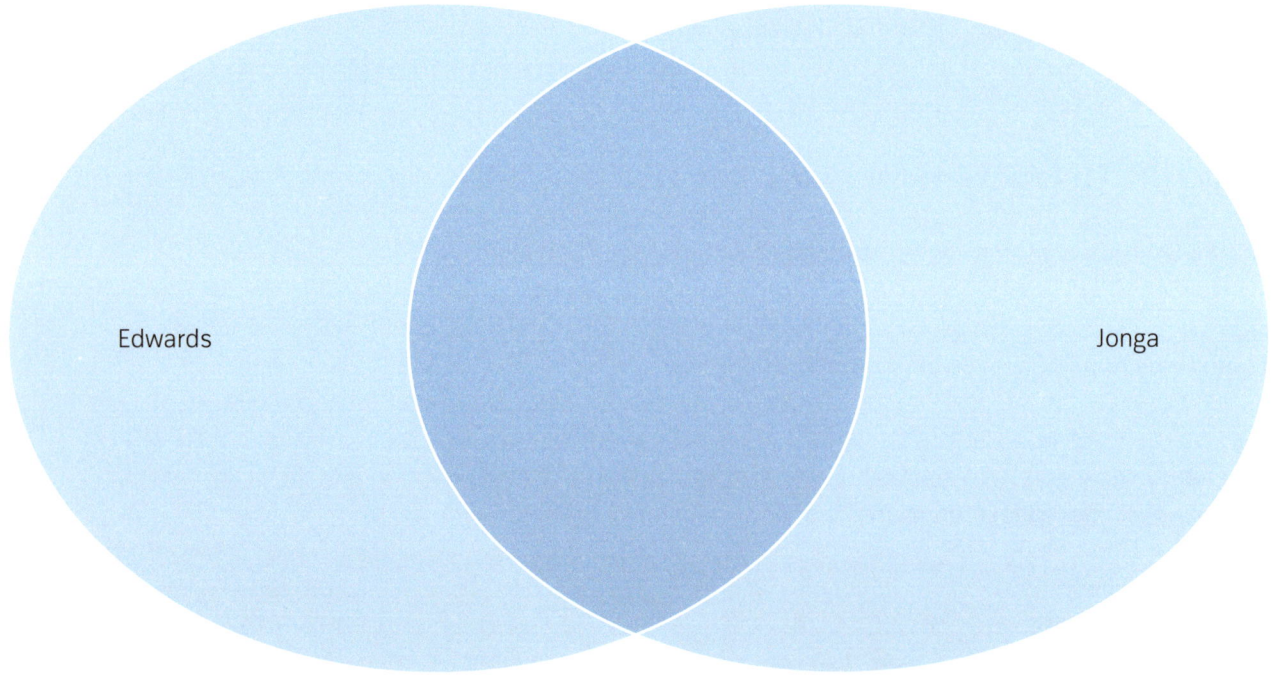

Edwards   Jonga

32

Compare Jende's to Neni's relationship with the Edwards family.

33

Describe the role of the church community for Neni and her family.

34

Examine the role of women in the novel.

35 → **S15:** How to describe pictures

a) Look at the two photos below. Describe the pictures and relate them to the novel.

1

2

b) Discuss whether the depiction of Clark and Jende in the novel reinforces stereotypes.

36

a) Discuss the thematic focus of the novel. Is the novel about …?

> immigration | finances | dreams | social class | equality | racism | the pursuit of happiness

b) Compare your findings to your expectations from task 1 on p. 34. Decide which book cover you think is most suitable to convey what the novel is about. Give reasons for your choice.

c) Create your own book cover based on your assessment.

37

a) Read the following text by Aaron Bady and outline his critique.

Has Imbolo Mbue Written the Great American Novel?
How an Unknown Cameroonian Novelist Followed in the Footsteps of Jonathan Franzen

By Aaron Bady   October 26, 2016

[…] At the start of the novel, Africa is given as a place to flee, an abjection to be abjured. When his employer idly asks him what his home village is like, he [Jende Jonga] is damningly unequivocal:

5   Everyone wants to come to America, sir. Everyone. To be in this country, sir. To live in

this country. Ah! It is the greatest thing in the world … my country is no good. It is nothing like America. I stay in my country, I would have become nothing. I would have remained nothing. My son will grow up and remain poor like me, just like I was poor like my father. But in America, sir? I can become something. I can

even become a respectable man. My son can
15 be a respectable man.

His dream of America, then, is this very particular
story of Obama: the dream that the son of an African might cease to be African. Instead of becoming
nothing – instead of being reduced to being a func-
20 tion of his own lies – he might become *something*.

The extent to which Jende Jonga buys into this version of the American dream – America as Not-Africa
– makes the novel, frankly, a bit racist. To put it
bluntly, it confirms and displays an uncomfortably
25 large number of stereotypes about Africa and Afri-
cans. If you make a list of words to describe Jende
Jonga, you get an image of the African as: simple,
good, hopeless, ignorant, confused, earnest, happy,
selfless, patriarchal, incurious, faithful, dependable,
30 and dependent. If he is sympathetic, the depth
of his pathos is matched and facilitated by his
shallowness of intellect; his American dream is
always, also, his totalizing self-negation as African.
He is many things, but one of them is a figure of
35 Fanonian[1] abjection; if his is the story of the American dream, it is also the story of African self-hate.

To be clear: Jende Jonga and his wife, Neni, are
rendered with sympathy and warmth, and it is their
lives which concern us as readers. But they are also
40 caricatures of the good-hearted, ignorant immigrant.
Their misconceptions about America are played
throughout for light comedy – as when Neni
describes lingerie as the American version of love
potions – and the many small confusions and humi-
45 liations which form Jende's life as a rich man's chauffeur never result in anything approaching resentment
or hostility. His love for his employer – and the depth
of his gratitude and satisfaction – is unsettling.

But maybe it's meant to be. I don't know. A carica-
50 ture can be warm-hearted, coming from a place of
sympathy and love. It can also be minstrelsy[2]. And
this is the question, the problem with the novel:
is it "problematic," or does it expose the problem
with the American dream, and its exceptionalist
55 presumptions? Without Obama's claim that "in
no other country on earth is my story even pos-

sible" – a line in his 2004 convention speech which
panders to soft racism and xenophobia – would his
presidency have been thinkable?

60 To believe in that American story – as Jende Jonga
wholeheartedly does, at the beginning of the novel
– one must accept its racist premise: to become a
person with an American future, Jende Jonga must
scrub away his African past. He must insist that
65 America *is* the promised land, for which he would
give anything; Africa is the bondage in Egypt from
which his family must flee. And so he does.

But this is not where the novel ends. What saves
it, for me, is the distance *Behold the Dreamers*
70 eventually creates between its subjects and their
dreams, between the dream they think they are
living and the lives they ultimately wake up to. It
does this through a simple act of narrative framing:
we never leave the minds of the novel's African
75 protagonists. For all its apparent fascination with a
rich, white, American-born family – as our protagonists eavesdrop and peer into the lives they
aspire to live – the book never leaves the perspective of their servants, never sees the one percent
80 except from the perspective of their employees; for
all the hyper-American signifiers that get thrown
around – immigration, the American dream, even
New York City itself – the novel only ever sees
America through their eyes. We never see the drea-
85 mers through America's.

This is important. Who is laughing clarifies who this
comedy of manners and errors is laughing *with*.
There is gentle mockery, here, of their pretensions
and misconceptions – as when Neni aspires,
90 someday, to purchase a fine suit from "a fine white
people store" like Target – but the naiveté of their
aspirations to nouveau riches is also their innocent
belief in America itself. And the novel ultimately
mocks both beliefs as naïve. Imbolo Mbue became
95 an American success story when she wrote this
novel, but her novel never tells this story. Jende
Jonga's son will not grow up to be Obama.

Instead, the novel uses the destruction of a family
to represent the failure of the American dream.

Annotations
1 **Fanonian** = relating to Frantz Fanon (1925–1961), French-Martiniquais psychologist and philosopher
2 **minstrelsy** = A minstrel was a travelling musician and singer in medieval times. The term can also refer to minstrel shows, in which white performers
  wore dark make-up to imitate black people through stereotypes and caricatures. (For more information cf. the box on p. 69.)

100 But the family that splinters is not Jende Jonga's: while the lives of the one percent fall apart, Jende Jonga's story continues even *after* its American chapter comes to a conclusion. [...] life is about irresolution, about questions, about change. And 105 [...] this novel ends with a question mark (literally) and with the question of what is to come next.

Behold the Dreamers is about the consequences of dreaming too long, too recklessly, and too credulously, but even more, it's about waking up from 110 that dream, and living, [...]. In the warm comedy of an immigrant family, we find a different story, a story that in its very irresolution, continues to have a future.

b) Comment on Aaron Bady's review. → **Workshop:** Writing a comment → **S6:** How to write a discussion/comment

38

a) You are a German student spending a year abroad in America. You have read the novel *Behold the Dreamers* in your high school literature class. Your teacher has asked the class to submit articles which show how the novel was received internationally. You have chosen an article from the German newspaper *FAZ*. Read the text below and use the information to write an English article in which you outline the strengths and weaknesses of the novel. → **Workshop:** Mediation → **S19:** How to improve your mediation skills

Imbolo Mbues neuer Roman

So hat Amerika die Einwanderer immer gebraucht

In „Das geträumte Land" bricht die Autorin Imbolo Mbue mit dem Klischee des amerikanischen Traums. Nun erscheint ihr in Amerika gefeierter Debütroman auf Deutsch. Eine Begegnung.

Von Annabelle Hirsch – 11.02.2017 – Aktualisiert am 15.02.2017, 13:17 Uhr

In der Nacht der amerikanischen Wahl saß Imbolo Mbue vor ihrem Fernseher in New York und schrie: „No! Florida! What's wrong with you?", „Iowa! OMG! What are you doing?", „Michigan, please don't!" Sie 5 zitterte und wütete, beschimpfte das Gerät, ging zu Bett und beschloss, erst einmal gar nicht mehr zu reden. Vielleicht weil man der Realität ihre Wirkungskraft ganz gut verweigert, solange man sie nicht benennt, vielleicht aber auch einfach weil, 10 na ja, worüber auch? Mit welchen Worten erfasst man eine Wirklichkeit, der man bis vor kurzem keine Chance eingeräumt hat?

Es sei ja gar nicht so, dass man es sich nicht hätte denken können, sagt sie, als wir uns zehn Tage 15 nach der Wahl an einem regnerischen Vormittag im „Whole Foods" des Times Warner Center in Manhattan treffen. Natürlich habe sie es irgendwie auch geahnt, so wie retrospektiv die meisten, aber man habe eben gehofft: „Wir hätten unseren Mäd-20 chen sagen können: Schau, eine Frau im Weißen Haus!" Die Tatsache, dass das Land, in das sie all ihre Hoffnung und Liebe gesteckt hat, dieses Land, in das sie vor über zehn Jahren aus ihrem kamerunischen Heimatort Limbé gekommen ist, um ein

25 besseres Leben zu finden, nun einen Mann wählt, der Menschen wie sie, also Frauen, Schwarze, Einwanderer, beschimpft und verachtet, sei ziemlich bitter. Die Tatsache, dass dieses Land, an das sie glaubt, offensichtlich an einen Mann wie 30 Donald Trump glaubt und ihn zum 45. Präsident der Vereinigten Staaten von Amerika macht, wiederum sehr ernüchternd.

Noch ein paar Wochen zuvor hatte Mbue in der „New York Times" darüber geschrieben, wie 35 glücklich und stolz sie sei, nach all den Jahren auf amerikanischem Boden endlich dazuzugehören, endlich Amerikanerin zu sein, endlich wählen zu können, überhaupt zum ersten Mal in ihrem Leben (in Kamerun zu wählen sei ziemlich witzlos). Und 40 darüber, wie komplex es dann aber auch sei, es zu tun, die konkurrierenden Gefühle der „von woanders Gekommenen" und der „Dazugehörenden", den Wunsch nach Offenheit mit dem nach Schutz in Einklang zu bringen: „Während die Bürgerin in 45 mir versteht, dass Amerika nicht jedem Einwanderer die Möglichkeiten geben kann, die er sich wünscht, und auch, dass Amerika sich erst einmal um Amerikaner kümmern muss, hofft die Ein-

wanderin in mir auf Gesetze, die Amerika als den
50 ,Traum, den Träumer träumten' erhält."
Über diesen Traum oder, besser gesagt, über die,
wie sie meint, bis heute ungebrochene Anziehungs-
kraft der Marke „American Dream" hat Imbolo
Mbue ein Buch, ihr erstes, geschrieben: „Behold
55 the Dreamers", das jetzt in Deutschland unter dem
etwas uninspiriert trockenen Titel „Das geträumte
Land" erscheint. Es wurde in den Vereinigten Staaten im vergangenen Herbst als Überraschungs-
erfolg gefeiert, „the one book Donald Trump should
60 read right now". Zum einen, weil Mbue für diesen
Erstlingsroman einen Vorschuss von einer Million
Euro bekommen hatte, was Berichterstatter fast
immer begeistert, auch wenn es über den Roman
nicht viel mehr sagt, als dass er einen guten Agen-
65 ten hatte (in dem Fall eine gute Agentin, nämlich
die von Jonathan Franzen). Zum anderen, weil sie
einen Nerv der Zeit getroffen hatte – und das auf
sehr kluge, differenzierte Art und Weise.

Für kurze Zeit vereint

70 Mbue erzählt in ihrem Roman die Geschichte der
Jongas, die von Jende, seiner Frau Neni und ihrem
Sohn Liomi, einer Einwandererfamilie aus Limbé,
Kamerun, die in New York im Jahr 2008 ihr Glück
und eine dauerhafte Aufenthaltsgenehmigung
75 suchen. Jende arbeitet als Chauffeur für den
Lehmann-Brothers-Top-Manager, Clark Edwards,
Neni studiert in der Hoffnung, irgendwann Apothe-
kerin zu werden, arbeitet nebenbei als Putzfrau
und einen idyllischen Sommer lang als Haushälte-
80 rin im Wochenend-Hamptons-Haus der Edwards.
Sie sind arm, sie haben es nicht leicht, aber sie
sind gewillt, hart zu arbeiten und alles zu tun für
ihren Traum: Einem Leben in Amerika, dem
„greatest country on earth", wie Jende Jonga, im
85 Einklang mit Barack Obamas letztem Video, seinem
Chef auf langen Autofahrten durch Manhattan
immer wieder mit glänzenden Augen erklärt.
Fast zwei Jahre lang scheint es, als würde alles gut
ausgehen. Die Jongas und die Edwards brauchen
90 sich, so wie Amerika seine Einwanderer immer
brauchte. Das jeweilige Glück der Familien hängt,
wenn auch in sehr unterschiedlicher existentieller
Gewichtung, voneinander ab. In dieser Zeit wird
auch noch Obama zum ersten schwarzen Präsi-
95 denten der Vereinigten Staaten gewählt, nichts
kann mehr schiefgehen, denken die Jongas und
träumen natürlich noch mehr, hören gar nicht

mehr hin, wenn der Cousin erklärt, in Amerika sei
die Polizei nur für weiße Mitbürger da, nicht für
100 die schwarzen, wenn einer ganz visionär erzählt,
irgendwann würde es eine Mauer geben und die
Mexikaner stünden dann nur noch dumpf drein-
schauend davor. Jende und Neni ignorieren diese
Warnungen und denken bei aller Vorsicht schon
105 fast, sie gehörten wirklich dazu. Zumindest kurz.
Denn dann kommt der Wall-Street-Crash, und die
Verzahnung der Leben dieser beiden so gegen-
sätzlichen Familien zerbricht.

Märchen versus Realität

110 So zusammengefasst erzählt, mag das Ganze
wie eine unerträgliche Anhäufung von Klischees
klingen. Wie das Märchen vom guten Wilden und
dem herzlosen Kapitalisten. Man könnte versucht
sein, Imbolo Mbues Roman für eine Anklageschrift
115 gegen die Amerikaner zu halten, die den Fremden
akzeptieren, solange er ihnen nützt, und ihn weg-
schmeißen, sobald er lästig wird. Nur umgeht die
Autorin diese Falle mühelos. Denn auch wenn sie
kaum verbergen kann (oder will), dass ihr Herz für
120 die Jongas schlägt, die aus ihrer Heimatstadt kommen, wie sie sprechen, wie sie essen und erleben,
was sie erlebt hat, sind die Figuren, die sie sehr
liebevoll, niemals grob, niemals urteilend zeichnet,
allesamt weder gut noch böse, sondern beides
125 zugleich. Alle versuchen das Richtige zu tun, aber
verzweifeln an diesem amerikanischen Traum, der
„größer als das Leben" ist, der alles verspricht und
es nur für wenige hält.
Manche Leser hätten ihr das vorgeworfen, sagt
130 Mbue, sie wollten lieber das Klischee. Sie hätten
zum Beispiel nicht akzeptiert, dass Jende, dem
man zuerst als gutherzigem Vater und Ehemann
begegnet, irgendwann gewalttätig wird, weil er sich
schämt, seiner Familie nicht mehr bieten zu kön-
135 nen, weil die Ungerechtigkeit der Realität ihn bricht.
Sie sage dann nur: „Männer aus meiner Stadt sind
eben leider so." Nur geht es am Ende vielleicht weniger darum, wie Männer aus ihrem Dorf sind oder
nicht sind, als darum, was bestimmte soziale und
140 geschichtliche Situationen mit Menschen machen.
Mit allen. Das wirklich Gute an Mbues Roman, der
sich ein bisschen wie ein Traum artikuliert, in dem
sich anfangs alles weich und beschützt anfühlt und
die Geräusche der Außenwelt immer mehr stören,
145 bis man schließlich aufwacht, liegt im Realismus,
mit dem sie dieser Frage begegnet.

Ihre Figuren, die man übrigens alle sehr mag, zeigen sich anfangs kämpferisch und guten Willens, hoffnungsvoll und gerecht, können sich
150 vor den Ängsten, die sie heimsuchen, aber nicht schützen. Da ist zum Beispiel Cindy Edwards, die hinter ihrer perfekten Fifth-Avenue-Society-Lady-Fassade noch immer darunter leidet, aus einem armen, gewalttätigen Elternhaus zu kommen, und
155 die den Absturz so sehr fürchtet, dass sie ihre Gutherzigkeit dabei vergisst. Oder Fatou, Nenis Freundin, die zwar in New York bleiben darf, sich aber irgendwann fragt, ob ihre Kinder, die Amerikaner sind, sich vielleicht insgeheim schämen, weil
160 sie Afrikanerin ist, und sich deshalb stärker an ihre Herkunftskultur klammert.

Statt sich ausufernd darauf zu konzentrieren, was den Einwanderer und den vermeintlichen „Native" unterscheidet, findet Imbolo Mbue ihre Gemein-
165 samkeiten, nämlich ihre Träume. Und entschuldigt damit auch vieles. Überhaupt scheint sie, die nach dem Börsencrash ihren Job verlor und damals, als sie schon fast daran dachte, nach Kamerun zurückzukehren, begann, an ihrem Roman zu
170 schreiben, weniger kämpferisch als verständnisvoll. Sie findet es zum Beispiel nicht mehr schlimm, wenn irgendwelche Damen kreischen: „Wie toll! Die Tochter einer Freundin war letztens in Süd-

afrika!", wenn sie sagt, sie komme aus Kamerun.
175 Ja, das sei, als würde man einem Franzosen sagen: „Wie schön! Ich war mal in Polen!" Aber was soll's.

Vertrauen in Amerika

Sie findet es auch nicht schlimm, zu wissen, dass sie immer, auch wenn sie mittlerweile einen ameri-
180 kanischen Pass besitzt, Schriftstellerin ist, ein gutes, integriertes Leben führt, in erster Linie eine Einwanderin bleiben wird: „Es ist ganz egal, wie lange ich hier bleibe, ob ich meinen Akzent verliere, ich werde immer von woanders gekommen sein.
185 Und wenn ich es mal vergesse, weiß ich es spätestens wieder, wenn man mich nach meiner Herkunft fragt." Viel wichtiger sei doch, dass sie Vertrauen in Amerika und seine „greatness" hat. Auch jetzt noch, auch wenn sie damit etwas ganz anderes
190 meint als Donald Trump.

Natürlich sei sie besorgt, nur hätten sich Sorgen und Ängste in der Geschichte noch nie als besonders gute Ratgeber erwiesen. Es sei an der Zeit, sich zu fragen, was sich die Menschen erhoffen,
195 und zu verstehen, wie weit entfernt die Realisierung ihrer Wünsche scheinen muss, um so einen Wahlausgang möglich zu machen: „Wir mögen zwar nicht mit ihnen einverstanden sein, aber wir sollten ihre Träume ernst nehmen."

b) Write your own review of the novel. → **S8:** How to improve your text

_____

_____

_____

_____

_____

_____

_____

_____

_____

The American Dream: Freedom, equality and the pursuit of happiness

a) What do you associate with the American Dream? Make a mind map.

The American Dream

b) Analyse the following quotes.

1 "[...] the American dream that has lured tens of millions of all nations to our shores in the past century has not been a dream of material plenty, though that has doubtless counted heavily. It has been much more than that. It has been a dream of being able to grow to fullest development as man and woman, unhampered by the barriers which had slowly been erected in older civilizations, unrepressed by social orders which had developed for the benefit of classes rather than for the simple human of any and every class."
– *James Truslow Adams (1878–1949), American writer and historian who coined the term "American Dream" in his book* The Epic of America *(1931).*

2 "We hold these truths to be self-evident, that all men are created equal, that they are endowed by their Creator with certain unalienable Rights, that among these are Life, Liberty and the pursuit of Happiness."
– *United States Declaration of Independence, In Congress, July 4, 1776*

3 "We don't see any American dream. We've experienced only the American nightmare."
– *Malcolm X (1925–1965), American activist and supporter of Black empowerment, was a prominent figure during the civil rights era; he gave his speech "The Ballot or the Bullet" in Detroit on April 12, 1964.*

4 "The reason they call it the American Dream is because you have to be asleep to believe in it."
– *George Carlin (1937–2008), American comedian, actor and social critic*

5 "Barack knows the American Dream because he's lived it ... and he wants everyone in this country to have that same opportunity, no matter who we are, or where we're from, or what we look like, or who we love."
– *Michelle Obama, First Lady of the United States from 2009 to 2017, giving a speech at the Democratic National Convention in Charlotte, N.C. on September 4, 2012. Barack Obama, 44th President of the United States, was the first African-American president in history.*

6

"So even though we face the difficulties of today and tomorrow, I still have a dream. It is a dream deeply rooted in the American dream. I have a dream that one day this nation will rise up and live out the true meaning of its creed: We hold these truths to be self-evident, that all men are created equal. [...]

I have a dream that my four little children will one day live in a nation where they will not be judged by the color of their skin but by the content of their character. I have a dream today."

– Martin Luther King Jr. (1929–1968), "I Have a Dream", speech delivered during the March on Washington for Jobs and Freedom on August 28, 1963; Martin Luther King Jr. fought against racial segregation and discrimination and was one of the most prominent leaders in the American civil rights movement.

c) Add new aspects to your mind map above.

2

a) The promise of equality is an integral element of the concept of the American Dream. Read the definition from the online encyclopedia *Britannica*. Then state what areas of life and parts of society 'equality' affects.

Info

Equality

Generally, an ideal of uniformity in treatment or status by those in a position to affect either. Acknowledgment of the right to equality often must be coerced from the advantaged by the disadvantaged. Equality of opportunity was the founding creed of U.S. society, but equality among all peoples and between the sexes has proved easier to legislate than to achieve in practice. [...]

---

b) Imagine that you have spent a year in the US and you are surprised at your perception of the reality of the American Dream. You have found an article in the German newspaper *Süddeutsche Zeitung* that seems to be in line with what you experienced, and you want to share the main points about social inequality in the US in an English blog post. Read the article below and use the information to write the blog post.

→ **Workshop:** Mediation   → **S19:** How to improve your mediation skills   → **S7:** Checklist: Writing a blog post

Soziale Gerechtigkeit
Die Illusion vom amerikanischen Traum

- In zwei Studien wurde untersucht, wie sich der Lebensstandard von Familien in den USA entwickelt hat.
- Sie zeigen: Das Versprechen vom sozialen Aufstieg gilt längst nicht mehr für jeden, und auch die Umverteilung durch den Staat bleibt weitgehend wirkungslos.

Von Catherine Hoffmann   27. Januar 2017, 20:00 Uhr

Der Glaube an den amerikanischen Traum ist angeschlagen. Die Wahl von Donald Trump zum US-Präsidenten wird von vielen Wissenschaftlern als die Rache der Abgehängten interpretiert, die
5 verbittert darüber sind, dass die Einkommensungleichheit seit Ausbruch der Finanzkrise im Jahr 2008 zugenommen hat. Trotz guter Wirtschaftszahlen haben die meisten amerikanischen Arbeiter und große Teile der Mittelschicht das Gefühl, dass
10 ihr Lebensstandard stagniert, während sich die Lage der Besserverdiener schnell erholt hat.

Zwei beachtliche Studien über die Entwicklung von Einkommen und Vermögen in den USA zeigen nun, dass dieses Gefühl nicht von ungefähr
15 kommt. Die Autoren zeichnen ein umfassendes Bild der sozialen Ungleichheit, die sich nicht erst mit der jüngsten Wirtschaftskrise verschärfte, sondern seit Generationen wächst. „The Fading American Dream" haben sechs Wissenschaftler
20 aus Stanford und Harvard über ihr Papier geschrieben, der verblassende amerikanische Traum.

Gemeint ist der Traum von einem Land, in dem das Leben für alle „besser und reicher und voller" sein sollte, wie es der amerikanische Publizist James Truslow Adams in seinem 1931 veröffentlichten Buch „The Epic of America" formulierte. Dieser Glaube, dass es jeder – wenn er nur hart genug dafür arbeitet – nach oben schaffen kann, hat die Vereinigten Staaten von Anfang an zusammengehalten. In den Jahrzehnten nach der Großen Depression wurde dieser Traum Wirklichkeit. Ein ungewöhnlich starkes Wirtschaftswachstum verbesserte den Lebensstandard aller Amerikaner, egal ob sie reich oder arm waren oder der Mittelschicht angehörten. 92 Prozent aller Kinder, die im Jahr 1940 in einem durchschnittlichen Haushalt geboren wurden, verdienten mit 30 Jahren mehr als ihre Eltern mit 30 verdient hatten. Auch den Kindern, denen dies nicht gelang, ging es oftmals gut: Sie waren nicht selten in einem reichen Haushalt aufgewachsen, der Vater Vorstand in einem Unternehmen, und arbeiteten selbst als Ärzte, Anwälte oder Professoren.

40 Jahre später gilt das Versprechen vom Aufstieg nicht mehr für alle: Nur die Hälfte der Kinder, die im Jahr 1980 geboren wurden, verdiente später mehr als ihre Eltern. „Im Grunde entscheidet ein Münzwurf, ob es einem besser geht als den Eltern", sagt Raj Chetty, Wirtschaftsprofessor und einer der Studienautoren. Aus dem Jahrgang 1950 gelang es immerhin noch fast 80 Prozent, den Wohlstand der Eltern zu übertreffen. Die Generationen der 1960 und 1970 Geborenen verwirklichten noch zu rund 60 Prozent die Hoffnungen auf ein besseres Leben. Der amerikanische Traum verblasst tatsächlich. Die Chance auf Teilhabe und Glück ist längst nicht mehr für alle Amerikaner gleich. Angesichts dieser Zahlen muss es niemanden überraschen, dass sich schleichend über viele Jahre und Jahrzehnte Frust aufgebaut hat. [...]

Es kommt also weniger auf das Wachstum als vielmehr auf die Verteilung des erreichten Wohl-stands an, will man das Versprechen vom Aufstieg der Fleißigen und Tüchtigen auch in der Gegenwart einlösen. Wie stark die Ungleichheit in den USA zugenommen hat, belegt auch eine Studie von Thomas Piketty, Emmanuel Saez und Gabriel Zucman. Die Wissenschaftler haben dafür nicht nur die Einkommen in den Blick genommen, sondern auch die Auswirkungen von Besteuerung, Sozial-ausgaben sowie die Einkünfte aus Kapitalanlagen. Ergebnis: Der Anteil der schlechter verdienenden Hälfte der amerikanischen Bevölkerung am Natio-naleinkommen verharrt seit 1980 bei etwa 16 000 Dollar (vor Steuern). Das Einkommen der unteren Schichten stagniert also seit zwei Jahrzehnten.

In derselben Zeit steigerte der Durchschnitt der Amerikaner seinen Anteil um 60 Prozent auf 64 500 Dollar, während das eine Prozent der Spitzenverdiener sein Kuchenstück von 420 000 auf 1,3 Millionen Dollar vergrößern konnte. Das führt dazu, dass das Nationaleinkommen 2014 unglei-cher verteilt ist als 1980: Der Anteil der schlechter verdienenden Bevölkerungshälfte schrumpfte von 20 auf zwölf Prozent, gleichzeitig schnellte der Anteil des einen Prozent der Spitzenverdiener am Nationaleinkommen von zwölf auf 20 Prozent.

Auch wenn man Steuern und Sozialleistungen berücksichtigt, ändert sich überraschend wenig an diesem Bild. Staatliche Umverteilung bleibt also weitgehend wirkungslos. Als wichtigsten Grund für die zunehmende Ungleichheit in jüngster Zeit machen die Ökonomen den rasanten Anstieg der Kapitaleinkünfte seit Ende der Neunzigerjahre aus, der vor allem den Spitzenverdienern zugutekam, die große Aktien- und Rentendepots besitzen.

Die neuen Studien erschüttern einmal mehr den Mythos von der sozialen Durchlässigkeit der amerikanischen Gesellschaft. Arbeit ist in den USA längst kein Garant mehr für Wohlstand und Gerechtigkeit, wie Adams noch gedacht hatte.

3

Read the interview with author Imbolo Mbue (on pp. 266–269, after the end of the novel) and summarize her story.

4

Is the American Dream dead?

a) Use the grid below to collect arguments that support the idea that the American Dream is dead and arguments that support the idea that the American Dream is alive.

b) Group work Use your arguments to discuss the question.

Is the American Dream dead?	
For (✔)	Against (✗)

FREEDOM, EQUALITY AND THE PURSUIT OF HAPPINESS IN *BEHOLD THE DREAMERS*

5

a) Pair work The Declaration of Independence acknowledges the right to "the pursuit of happiness", which is an essential part of the concept of the American Dream. Define what happiness means to you.

b) Explain what happiness means for the characters in *Behold the Dreamers*.

6

Examine the relationship between Jende and Clark with respect to the concept of equality.

7

Describe the perceptions and experiences of the American Dream by the following characters:
- Vince Edwards
- Clark Edwards
- Jende Jonga
- Cindy Edwards
- Neni Jonga

8 → **S23:** How to quote → **S8:** How to improve your text

Compare the points made in Catherine Hoffmann's article "Die Illusion vom amerikanischen Traum" (p. 49f.) to the perceptions of the American Dream in the novel.

9

Compare Jende and Neni's immigration story to Imbolo Mbue's.

10 → **S23:** How to quote → **S8:** How to improve your text

Explain how the novel can be described as "a dissection of the American dream" (as Carmela Ciuraru phrased it in her 2016 article in *The New York Times*).

Questions of identity

1   Group work

a)   Try to define 'identity'.

Method: Placemat

Get into groups of four and divide a big sheet of paper (in A3 format) as shown on the right.

Step 1: Try to solve the task by yourself first and write down your results in your section.

Step 2: Rotate the sheet and read each other's outcomes.

Step 3: Decide on a definition together and write it down in the middle.

Info

b)   Visualize your results and present them in class.

c)   Which aspects do you find most important? Rank them and explain your choices.

IDENTITY IN *BEHOLD THE DREAMERS*

Analyse what parts of Neni's and Jende's identities are stressed in the novel.

3

Comment on the quotes below.

> She'd waited too long to become something, and now, at thirty-three, she finally had, or was close enough to having, everything she'd ever wanted in life.
> *(narrator about Neni, p. 15)*

> "It is nothing like America. I stay in my country, I would have become nothing. I would have remained nothing. My son will grow up and be poor like me, just like I was poor like my father. But in America, sir? I can become something. [...]"
> *(Jende to Clark, p. 32)*

> "[...] And my son will grow up to be somebody, whatever he wants to be. [...]"
> *(Jende to Clark, p. 37)*

> "[...] Without school, you will be nothing. You will never be anybody. Me and Papa, we wake up every day and do everything we can so you can have a good life and become somebody one day, [...]"
> *(Neni to Liomi, p. 50)*

> Jende was going to be somebody in Limbe when they returned.
> *(narrator about Jende, p. 242)*

The financial crisis

Watch a video about the Great Recession and answer the questions below.   **Webcode**   DSW-73699-03

a)   What are subprime mortgages and what is their significance to the financial crisis?

_____

_____

_____

b) What was the development in the housing market before 2007?

_____

_____

_____

c) What happened to the housing market after 2007?

_____

_____

_____

d) How did the bursting of the housing bubble affect the banks, the economy and people in America?

2

Read the article from *The New York Times* and outline the present and possible future consequences of the financial crisis.

From Trump to Trade, the Financial Crisis Still Resonates 10 Years Later

By Andrew Ross Sorkin   September 10, 2018

This week is the 10th anniversary of the inflection point of the financial crisis: the collapse of Lehman Brothers, the biggest bankruptcy in history. To some, it feels like a long time ago.

5 Yet, its effects still echo in the way we live today – in the attitudes that pervade our economy, our culture and our politics. It is hardly a stretch to suggest that President Trump's election was a direct result of the financial crisis.

10 The crisis was a moment that cleaved our country. It broke a social contract between the plutocrats[1] and everyone else. But it also broke a sense of trust, not just in financial institutions and the government that oversaw them, but in the very idea of experts and 15 expertise. The past 10 years have seen an open revolt against the intelligentsia.

Mistrust led to new political movements: the Tea Party for those who didn't trust the government and Occupy Wall Street for those who didn't trust big 20 business. These moved Democrats and Republicans away from each other in fundamental ways, and populist attitudes on both ends of the spectrum found champions in the 2016 presidential race in Senator Bernie Sanders and Donald J. Trump.

25 The depth of financial despair during the Great Recession and the invariably slow recovery have

Annotations   [1] **plutocrat** = sb who is powerful because they are rich

unleashed a sense of bitterness that dominates the political landscape, culminating in Mr. Trump's electoral victory.

30 "We are almost at each other's throats when times are good," said Ray Dalio, the founder of Bridgewater Associates, the largest hedge fund in the world with some $150 billion in assets, and the author of a new book, "A Template for Understanding Big Debt
35 Crises," an exhaustive study of financial panics and the policies that both created and rescued them.

The deepest crises, he said, always lead to populism. And it should be no surprise that a crisis leads to conflict and, in some extreme cases, war. "I would be
40 worried about the emergence of populism," he said, "because populists tend to want to fight with the other side rather than try to find ways of getting through it." Populists on every side of the political spectrum "have in common that they're confrontational," he said.

45 When I wrote "Too Big to Fail" nearly a decade ago, I knew that the crisis would redefine Wall Street and the economy, but I didn't appreciate how fundamentally it would redefine the political environment.

Amir Sufi, a professor of economics and public policy
50 at University of Chicago's Booth School of Business and the co-author of "House of Debt," pointed to the financial crisis as the source of reduced civility a few months after Mr. Trump's victory. He conducted an analysis of 60 countries with his "House of Debt"
55 co-author, Atif Mian of Princeton University, and Francesco Trebbi of the University of British Columbia. They found that such a response was "common and predictable," he wrote.

"Our conclusion: Financial crises tend to radicalize
60 electorates," Mr. Sufi wrote. "After a banking, currency, or debt crisis, our data indicate, the share of centrists or moderates in a country went down, while the share of left- or right-wing radicals went up in most cases."

In the United States, the crisis exposed an economy
65 that had been a charade – one that most Americans didn't understand or appreciate. The use of debt had masked the real problems underneath the surface: a significant decrease in worker participation, automation that would take jobs and stagnant wage
70 growth.

These issues long predated the crisis. But as Warren Buffett famously said, "You only find out who is swimming naked when the tide goes out."

In truth, our economy today is in much better shape
75 than you might expect, with unemployment at 3.9 percent – lower than it was before the crisis.

Yet debates persist about the way the government, first under President George W. Bush and then under President Barack Obama, chose to respond to the crisis.
80 Should it have done more directly for homeowners?

Should it have demanded more onerous terms for the hundreds of billions of dollars in loans to the banks and bankers, like restricting compensation and firing executives to demonstrate more accountability?
85 Should some bankers have gone to jail?

For some, it is tempting to think that the government should have taken a more populist approach itself. If it had offered more help directly to the public rather than what was perceived as bailing out the banks,
90 there is a suspicion that divisions could have been lessened, yielding a more united United States.

But would it?

In Britain, the government did all those politically popular things: It restricted banker pay, it fired
95 executives, it lent money to banks on onerous terms, it restricted spending.

It didn't work. The British economy grew significantly slower than ours. And the resulting resentment and bitterness were much worse than our own, leading to
100 a manifestation of populism even more drastic: the unimaginable vote to leave the European Union.

It's not popular to say, but it's clear that the financial crisis was so deep and so painful that whatever populist positions policymakers took, the positive
105 feelings would have been short-lived.

Timothy F. Geithner, the Treasury secretary under Mr. Obama, recounted in his book "Stress Test" a conversation that he had with President Bill Clinton as he was considering a more populist approach. Mr.
110 Clinton told him, "You could take Lloyd Blankfein into a dark alley, and slit his throat, and it would satisfy them for about two days. Then the blood lust would rise again."

It doesn't help that the economic medicine used by
115 policymakers after a crisis exacerbates those feelings of anger. The most efficient fix – lowering interest rates – helps the wealthy because they end up with cheaper mortgages and enjoy the benefits that low rates have on corporate growth. Those lower on
120 the economic ladder, on the other hand, get little in interest on their savings. The gap between the haves and the have-nots widens.

But that approach actually works, pulling everyone along with it, even if it is uneven and there are greater
125 beneficiaries than others.

There is one question I get more than any other: "Will we have another crisis?" The answer, of course, is yes. But it's not a Wall Street crisis similar to 2008 that concerns me. I'm worried about something far bigger.
130 When I wrote "Too Big to Fail," that phrase was only used in the context of financial institutions. Today, it is used to refer to cities, municipalities, states and countries. If you look at the buildup of debt, that's the place to keep an eye on.

Unmanageable debt is the match that lights the fire of every crisis. You can have as many bad actors on stage as you want – greedy bankers, inept regulators, conflicted credit rating agencies – but unless there is significant leverage in the system, there's little danger of a crisis. Our national debt is more than $21 trillion, and it increased a trillion dollars in just six months under Mr. Trump, who rode populist and anti-establishment sentiment to the White House but whose policy choices have largely favored the wealthy.

That's not the only cause for concern, either. If history tells us the political divisions we have seen since the financial crisis were predictable, then what does history have to say about what comes next?

Mr. Dalio pointed to the chilling of international relationships that happened after the Great Depression as a worrying example of the divisions that can widen when populism fosters protectionism. "We started to have economic tariffs and we started to have back-and-forths of those things," he said.

He paused for a moment, signaling he didn't want to contemplate what that later manifested. But he continued, "Which then, 10 years later, led to Pearl Harbor."

There are, of course, many steps between populism and war. But Mr. Dalio said he saw similarities between the global environment that preceded World War II and the one we see today.

That's reason enough to never forget this crisis and its lessons.

THE FINANCIAL CRISIS IN *BEHOLD THE DREAMERS*

3

Describe how the collapse of Lehman Brothers unfolds in the novel.

4

Relate Jende's dream about "money doublers" (pp. 119–120) in Limbe to the collapse of Lehman Brothers.

5

Examine the consequences of the financial crisis for the individual characters in the novel.

6

Imagine that Jende tries to explain to a friend in Limbe how the financial crisis began. Create a dialogue between the two of them.

Political, cultural and social developments

1 Group work

Choose one of the topics below and research the most important facts on the Internet to illustrate their general ideals.

- Democrats
- Republicans
- Barack Obama
- Donald Trump
- Joe Biden

— Info —

Method: Jigsaw

Five students research the same topic respectively, for example A. They form an expert group (e.g. A, A, A, A, A), exchange results and prepare them for a presentation. Then the students get together in mixed groups (A, B, C, D, E) and inform each other on their topics.

2 → **Workshop:** Analysing a speech → **S14:** How to analyse a speech

Analyse the extract from Barack Obama's speech "The American Promise" (2008).

Address Accepting the Presidential Nomination at the Democratic National Convention in Denver: "The American Promise"

August 28, 2008

[…] Four years ago, I stood before you and told you my story – of the brief union between a young man from Kenya and a young woman from Kansas who weren't well-off or well-known, but shared a belief
5 that in America, their son could achieve whatever he put his mind to.

It is that promise that has always set this country apart – that through hard work and sacrifice, each of us can pursue our individual dreams but still come
10 together as one American family, to ensure that the next generation can pursue their dreams as well.

That's why I stand here tonight. Because for two hundred and thirty-two years, at each moment when that promise was in jeopardy, ordinary men and
15 women – students and soldiers, farmers and teachers, nurses and janitors – found the courage to keep it alive.

We meet at one of those defining moments – a moment when our nation is at war, our economy is in turmoil,
20 and the American promise has been threatened once more.

Tonight, more Americans are out of work and more are working harder for less. More of you have lost your homes and even more are watching your home
25 values plummet. More of you have cars you can't afford to drive, credit card bills you can't afford to pay, and tuition that's beyond your reach.

[…] These are my heroes. Theirs are the stories that shaped me. And it is on their behalf that I intend
30 to win this election and keep our promise alive as President of the United States.

What is that promise?

It's a promise that says each of us has the freedom to make of our own lives what we will, but that we also
35 have the obligation to treat each other with dignity and respect.

It's a promise that says the market should reward drive and innovation and generate growth, but that businesses should live up to their responsibilities to
40 create American jobs, look out for American workers, and play by the rules of the road.

Ours is a promise that says government cannot solve all our problems, but behat it should do is that which we cannot do for ourselves – protect us from harm
45 and provide every child a decent education; keep our water clean and our toys safe; invest in new schools and new roads and new science and technology.

Our government should work for us, not against us. It should help us, not hurt us. It should ensure
50 opportunity not just for those with the most money and influence, but for every American who's willing to work.

That's the promise of America – the idea that we are responsible for ourselves, but that we also rise or fall
55 as one nation; the fundamental belief that I am my brother's keeper[1]; I am my sister's keeper.

That's the promise we need to keep. That's the change we need right now.

[…] Passions fly on immigration, but I don't know
60 anyone who benefits when a mother is separated from her infant child or an employer undercuts American wages by hiring illegal workers. This too is part of America's promise – the promise of a democracy where we can find the strength and grace to bridge
65 divides and unite in common effort.

I know there are those who dismiss such beliefs as happy talk. They claim that our insistence on something larger, something firmer and more honest in our public life is just a Trojan Horse for higher taxes
70 and the abandonment of traditional values. And that's to be expected. Because if you don't have any fresh ideas, then you use stale tactics to scare the voters. If you don't have a record to run on, then you paint your opponent as someone people should run from.
75 You make a big election about small things.

And you know what – it's worked before. Because it feeds into the cynicism we all have about government. When Washington doesn't work, all its promises seem empty. If your hopes have been dashed again
80 and again, then it's best to stop hoping, and settle for what you already know.

I get it. I realize that I am not the likeliest candidate for this office. I don't fit the typical pedigree, and I haven't spent my career in the halls of Washington.
85 But I stand before you tonight because all across America something is stirring. What the nay-sayers don't understand is that this election has never been about me. It's been about you.

For eighteen long months, you have stood up, one
90 by one, and said enough to the politics of the past.

Annotations
[1] This is a reference to the biblical story of Cain and Abel.

You understand that in this election, the greatest risk we can take is to try the same old politics with the same old players and expect a different result. You have shown what history teaches us – that at 95 defining moments like this one, the change we need doesn't come from Washington. Change comes to Washington. Change happens because the American people demand it – because they rise up and insist on new ideas and new leadership, a new politics for a 100 new time.

America, this is one of those moments. [...]

This country of ours has more wealth than any nation, but that's not what makes us rich. We have the most powerful military on Earth, but that's not what makes 105 us strong. Our universities and our culture are the envy of the world, but that's not what keeps the world coming to our shores.

Instead, it is that American spirit – that American promise – that pushes us forward even when the path 110 is uncertain; that binds us together in spite of our differences; that makes us fix our eye not on what is seen, but what is unseen, that better place around the bend.

That promise is our greatest inheritance. It's a promise 115 I make to my daughters when I tuck them in at night, and a promise that you make to yours – a promise that has led immigrants to cross oceans and pioneers to travel west; a promise that led workers to picket lines, and women to reach for the ballot.

120 And it is that promise that forty-five years ago today, brought Americans from every corner of this land to stand together on a Mall in Washington, before Lincoln's Memorial, and hear a young preacher from Georgia speak of his dream.[2]

125 The men and women who gathered there could've heard many things. They could've heard words of anger and discord. They could've been told to succumb to the fear and frustration of so many dreams deferred. But what the people heard instead – people of every 130 creed and color, from every walk of life – is that in America, our destiny is inextricably linked. That together, our dreams can be one.

"We cannot walk alone," the preacher cried. "And as we walk, we must make the pledge that we shall 135 always march ahead. We cannot turn back."

America, we cannot turn back. Not with so much work to be done. Not with so many children to educate, and so many veterans to care for. Not with an economy to fix and cities to rebuild and farms to save. Not 140 with so many families to protect and so many lives to mend. America, we cannot turn back. We cannot walk alone. At this moment, in this election, we must pledge once more to march into the future. Let us keep that promise – that American promise – and in the 145 words of Scripture hold firmly, without wavering, to the hope that we confess.

Thank you, God bless you, and God bless the United States of America.

Annotations

[2] This is a reference to Martin Luther King Jr. and his speech "I Have a Dream", which he gave during the March on Washington for Jobs and Freedom on August 28, 1963.

3

a) Describe the photos → **S15:** How to describe pictures

Info

January 6 U.S. Capitol attack, storming of the United States Capitol on January 6, 2021, by a mob of supporters of Republican Pres. Donald J. Trump. The attack disrupted a joint session of Congress convened to certify the results of the presidential election of 2020, which Trump had lost to his Democratic opponent, Joe Biden. Because its object was to prevent a legitimate president-elect from assuming office, the attack was widely regarded as an insurrection or attempted coup d'état. The Federal Bureau of Investigation (FBI) and other law-enforcement agencies also considered it an act of domestic terrorism. For having given a speech before the attack in which he encouraged a large crowd of his supporters near the White House to march to the Capitol and violently resist Congress's certification of Biden's victory – which many in the crowd then did – Trump was impeached by the Democratic-led House of Representatives for "incitement of insurrection" (he was subsequently acquitted by the Senate). [...] (From the online encyclopedia *Britannica*)

b) Analyse the cartoons. → **Workshop:** Analysing a cartoon → **S17:** How to work with cartoons

4

a) Go back to Annabelle Hirsch's article on p. 45ff. Summarize Imbolo Mbue's reaction to the presidential election of 2016, after which Donald Trump became the 45th President of the United States.

b) Identify the concept of identity that is revealed in her reaction.

c) Explain what Imbolo Mbue means by saying that the US needs to take care of Americans first.

d) Comment on the question of whether her hopes of America remaining 'the land of dreams' have come true.

5

Do some additional research on Donald Trump. Then comment on the title of Lucia Grave's 2016 article in *The Guardian*: "America's Trump nightmare has arrived".

6

Reread the information about equality in the box on p. 49. What kind of equality does the Black Lives Matter (BLM) movement envision?

7

Watch the video "Black Lives Matter – The history of a movement" from *Channel 4 News*.
Webcode DSW-73699-04
Answer the following questions about the BLM movement.

a) Which incident started the Black Lives Matter movement?

_____

_____

b) How did the slogan evolve?

_____

_____

c) What is the agenda of the BLM movement?

_____

_____

d) Where does the rallying cry "I can't breathe" originate from?

_____

_____

e) What happened in Ferguson?

_____

_____

_____

f) What measures were taken by the Obama administration?

_____

_____

g) What reasons are given for the police officers "getting away with murder"?

_____

_____

h) What consequences for the BLM movement were there under the Trump administration?

_____

_____

_____

8 → **Workshop:** Analysing a cartoon → **S17:** How to work with cartoons

Analyse the cartoons.

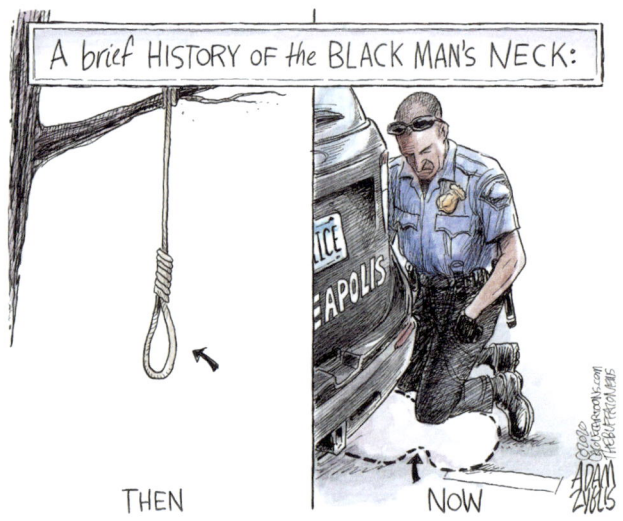

9

Watch two short extracts
(34:50–40:20 and 48:00–52:27)
from President Biden's address to Congress in 2021.

Webcode DSW-73699-05

Decide whether the statements below are true or false.

President Biden …		true	false
1	wants millionaires to pay their fair share of taxes.		
2	intends to reward work and not just wealth.		
3	plans to impose higher taxes on the middle class.		
4	is determined to grow the economy by supporting the middle class.		
5	remarks that the current pay gap between CEOs and their workers is extremely large.		
6	plans to fight white supremacy's terrorism.		
7	recounts that George Floyd's daughter said that her father had died in vain.		
8	believes that the trust in law enforcement needs to be re-established.		
9	vows to fight systemic racism, work towards real equity, and enable people to build generational wealth.		
10	supports the Equality Act to protect LGBTQ+ Americans.		

10

Compare the stances of Barack Obama, Donald Trump and Joe Biden on the major issues of immigration, integration and support of the middle class.

Stances on ...	Barack Obama	Donald Trump	Joe Biden
immigration			
integration			
the middle class			

POLITICAL, CULTURAL AND SOCIAL ISSUES IN *BEHOLD THE DREAMERS*

11

Summarize the differing attitudes of Americans and American institutions towards immigrants in the novel.

12

Reread the short extract from Martin Luther King's speech on p. 49. Comment on whether you think that Martin Luther King's dream has been realized in the fictional reality of the novel.

13

Examine the depiction of Barack Obama in the novel.

14

Compare Obama's "American promise" (cf. p. 56f.) and his vision of America with Neni's and Jende's initial perceptions of America.

15 CHOOSE

Imagine that Neni and Jende have observed the political developments in America and they have a conversation about Donald Trump's presidency. Write their dialogue.

OR

Imagine that Neni writes an email to Mighty and Vince commenting on the presidential election of 2020, after which Joe Biden became the 46th President of the United States. Write her email.

Pre-reading

Read the title of the play and The Premeditation. Speculate on what the play will be about.

2

a) Read the article from *The Standard* about the dramatist Jasmine Lee-Jones.

b) Find out more about her:
- age
- family background
- motivation for writing the play
- ideals
- personal experiences with theatre
- ...

Jasmine Lee-Jones interview: I want people to come to the theatre like they watch Netflix

by Jessie Thompson

[...] Jasmine Lee-Jones's debut play, exploring female friendship, cultural appropriation and the internet, became one of the most talked-about plays of the year after a triumphant run at the
5 Royal Court, picking up a trail of awards and an ecstatic stream of social media appreciation. [...]

It's immediately obvious when talking to Lee-Jones IRL, [...] that she is a deep and impressive thinker, often pausing for several seconds before
10 she answers a question. [...]

Born in North London, Lee-Jones became interested in theatre because of a strong connection she felt with words and language. "I always wanted to read things out loud," she says. "When I found theatre,
15 I started to realise: oh, you can do a job where you're actually paid to speak words aloud, to really interrogate language." [...]

The play's text is written in gifs, online acronyms, merging the IRL-world with the social media-
20 sphere. It's the most original and successful way any writer has ever managed to capture the internet on stage, but Lee-Jones didn't do it on purpose – she just wanted it to feel real. "I think theatre can sometimes feel quite isolating like, oh, this is for
25 someone else. We have a prestige about theatre and what should be on stage, like it's just for Shakespeare. And then you put something in from the internet that feels very casual and personal to people, and people are willing to give you more
30 license," she says. [...]

The online reaction to seven methods made it clear that the play was reaching new, more diverse audiences, something that matters greatly to Lee-Jones. "I want people to come to the theatre like they
35 watch Netflix," she says. "I like watching reality TV and all of that as much as the next person. But one thing I find super interesting about TV is everyone will watch good, really thoroughly written, well-plotted TV. [...] But when there's something really
40 good in theatre on, people still feel like it's not for them. There's a universality to TV and film that theatre just hasn't created yet. It's still like, oh, it's meant for those people." [...]

Having been nurtured as a writer by the Royal
45 Court from the age of 17, Lee-Jones has always felt more comfortable there than at other theatres. But she had an experience a few years ago that shook that. She was watching a play with a friend, also a black woman, and they were waiting at the bar
50 to get a drink. "This group of white people, I think maybe husband and wife, just went in front of us. I looked at my friend and was like, did you see that? And she just nodded, but eventually I realised they just didn't see us. They didn't think we were there
55 to do something important or watch a show. They thought we were kind of just loitering," she tells me. "I think that was the first experience I had in this theatre where I realised – not because of the theatre, necessarily – but there's an audience that
60 thinks this space belongs to them more than other people."

In the post-pandemic era, Lee-Jones thinks the theatre world will only bring in new audiences if it's really committed to doing so. "They have
65 to keep programming the plays until people feel safe enough to come to the work. And what happened to me in the bar downstairs doesn't keep happening, because people realise: oh, this space is for everyone, it's not just for us." As she's
70 telling me this, just behind her is the Royal Court's building; on the front of it, her name is written in neon lights. How thrilling that, right now, that one belongs to her. [...]

3   Pair work

a) State what you know about Kylie Jenner, an American media celebrity.
b) Find out more about her on the Internet and decide whether the statements below are true or false. Correct the false statements.

statement	true	false	correction
1. Kylie Jenner is the daughter of Caitlyn and Kris Jenner.			
2. Kylie Jenner belongs to the Generation Alpha.			
3. She was part of the reality TV series *Keeping Up with the Kardashians* because she was adopted by Robert Kardashian.			
4. Jenner launched her own cosmetics line called *Kylie's BW lip kit*.			
5. In 2017, she was placed on the *Forbes* Celebrity 100 list, which made her the youngest person to be featured on the list.			
6. Kylie Jenner beat Mark Zuckerberg by two years when being announced the youngest self-made billionaire in 2019.			
7. Kylie Jenner is black.			

Language

4

a) **Pair work / Group work** Social media users don't normally use formal language. What abbreviations do you use?

CHOOSE

Write down the abbreviations that you use.

OR

Use a digital tool to do this task.

b) Rewrite the following comment in Standard English.

> **INCOGNEGRO @INCOGNEGRO · Mar 5**
> Errybody and they aunty need to quit fronting like Kylie killing it! She ain't killing shit! And tbh if I had it my way the only thing getting kilt would be that bitch! #kyliejennerfidead (p. 5)

5

Reading social media content in another language can be confusing. All the slang, idioms and abbreviations people use can make even simple sentences tricky to understand.

a) Get acquainted with the abbreviations the protagonists use in the play. Match the meanings from the box to the correct abbreviations and write them into the table.

actually | big man ting (= seriously) | Don't piss me off! | Go on! | I don't care! | Kiss my teeth! | Never mind! | not gonna lie | Oh my days! | Say no more! | similar to LOL ✓ | Swear to God! | to be honest | What are you doing? | What the hell!

abbreviation	meaning
LEWL	*similar to LOL*
DPMO	
OMDS	
BMT	
IDC	
SNM	
S2G	
nvm	
wyd	
KMT	
ngl	
acc	
WTH	
tbh	
gwarn	

b) Now compare your results with the list of the most important abbreviations used in the play. You can find the list online. **Webcode** DSW-73699-06

c) While reading the play, add more abbreviations that are used by the protagonists to your list.

d) Rewrite the following email as a tweet by using as many abbreviations as possible.

> Hello, my best friend in the Twitter world!
> How are you today? I can't believe we're finally meeting each other. Have I told you that my mom believes you don't exist? That's extremely funny!!!!! However, I can't wait to meet you in real life. I'll see you in Berlin next week!
> Bye for now,
> your dearest friend

e) **CHALLENGE** You may add content to make the tweet sound more realistic.

f) **OPTIONAL** Rewrite the following hypothetical tweet into Standard English.

> Look @ her DP. What a QT! tbh, AFAIK – that's so fake! Never IRL! I'm BWL☺ Check X 4 more lies!
> And btw, DM next time!

While reading

Info

The media in a fast-changing world

In 2022, billionaire Elon Musk (founder of SpaceX and other companies, product architect of Tesla) bought the social networking service Twitter and became its CEO. The platform has subsequently been criticized for an increase in content containing disinformation and hate speech. In the summer of 2023, Elon Musk announced that the name of **Twitter**, which had been in use since 2006, would be changed to **X**. He also introduced a new logo and wanted to get rid of associated words such as "tweet".

Jasmine Lee-Jones made changes to her play and published a new version in 2021, only two years after the first publication in 2019. At the time of her second publication, Twitter with its original name was still in practice.

---

6 **CHOOSE**

Tip	Keeping a reading journal with the focus on summarizing the plot as well as adding information about the setting and relevant page numbers can be one option for remembering the content of a play. Taking notes with a specific focus (e.g. on one of the characters, topics, language, etc.) is another option to structure the content of a play.

Focus on one character's perspective: What aspects of Kylie's life are making Cleo furious? Take notes while reading.

OR

Focus on language: The playwright uses words from the black community, like "kiking" (p. 14), "bredrin" (p. 8), etc. Find more examples and explain their meanings.

OR

Focus on language: The play deals with serious topics but in a comical tone. Find examples from the text and evaluate the author's decision to make use of comic elements. Start a table like the one below and fill in your results.

quotation	topic	effect
1.		

THE PREMEDITATION (PP. 1–3)

7

a) Fill in the table.

1.	**Who** are the characters?	
2.	**When** do the scenes take place?	
3.	**Where** does the action take place?	
4.	**What** action is described?	
5.	**What** references are made to the world outside the stage?	

b) In the second version of her play from 2021, Jasmine Lee-Jones made considerable changes to The Premeditation from the original version from 2019 (see below). If you were Jasmine Lee-Jones and were asked by journalists why you made those changes to the play, apart from "A work of art is never finished" what would you answer?

> *The present.*
> *In the most present sense of the present tense.*
> *5th March 2019.*
> *Early morning. Outside. A park. Dark.*
>
> *KARA and CLEO drag something resembling a body onto the platform. They open the traps and throw it in. Cover it with earth. Suddenly they stop, standing over the body.*
>
> *Blackout.*

PART 1 (PP. 4–9): THE START

8

a) Cleo retweets a tweet by Forbes. Describe the Forbes tweet in your own words.

_____

b) Explain why Cleo is angry about the tweet.

_____

c) Cleo creates the hashtag #kyliejennerfidead as a response to the Forbes tweet and tweets hypothetical death threats against Kylie Jenner. Describe Cleo's methods in your own words.

Method #1: _____

Method #2: _____

d) Complete the sentence: With tweeting the first two methods of killing, Cleo wants to point out / criticize / make aware of the facts / aim at …

_____

e) Fill in the summary with the appropriate adjectives from the box.

> angry | crazy | happy | hypothetical |
> ingenious | real | surprise | worried

The first part of the plot describes developments in the Twitter world as well as in real life. When the action takes

place in _____ life, Cleo gets a _____ visit from Kara. Kara has seen Cleo's tweets

and wants to know why she is _____. Cleo plays down the seriousness of

her _____ death threats and therefore wants to calm her _____

friend.

PART 2 (PP. 10–27): TWITTERLUDE 1–2 AND IRL

9

Social media users are responding to Cleo's tweets (pp. 10–13).

a) **Pair work** List the words they are using.

_____

_____

b) Describe the tone of the tweets.

> **Info**
>
> ### Tone
>
> Tone refers to an author's use of words and writing style to convey his or her attitude towards a topic. Tone is transported through the choice of words, viewpoint, syntax (grammar, how you put words together) and level of formality.

Language support

Talking about tone

accusatory | admiring | aggressive | ambivalent | amused | appreciative | colloquial | concerned | critical | defensive | (dis)respectful | (dis)approving | judgmental | ...

_____

_____

c) Explain the following quote in the play's context:

"Inside that tweet is hundreds of years of anti-blackness, positive affirmations of capitalism, cultural appropriation ..." (p. 15)

d) Name and describe Method #3 in your own words.

_____

e) Describe the tone of the responses to Method #3.

_____

f) **Pair work** CHOOSE

Kara and Cleo have different opinions on various matters. They are having an argument about the importance of the tweet (p. 15). List their arguments.

Topic of discussion: "It's (just) a tweet."	
Kara	Cleo

OR

Kara and Cleo are having an argument about the application of violence as an answer to oppression (p. 21). List their arguments.

Topic of discussion: "Violence is the answer to oppression."	
Kara	Cleo

g) Cleo has broken up with her boyfriend. Explain why his new girlfriend upsets Cleo.

h) OPTIONAL

Pair work Act out the scene in which the two girls talk about Cleo's boyfriend, the breakup and the new girlfriend.

OR

Group work (4) Create a freeze-frame in which the relationships between the following characters become apparent: Cleo, Cleo's boyfriend, the new girlfriend and Kara. You may also add up to three sentences that each character is saying.

The protagonists

10 **Group work** CHOOSE

What do you get to know about Cleo when reading the play? Write down her profile.
Note down the pages where you found the information.

Age: _____

Education: _____

Family and friends: _____

Topics of interest: _____

Political views: _____

Sexual orientation: _____

Black identity (appearance, language, etc.): _____

Character traits: _____

OR

What do you get to know about Kara when reading the play? Write down her profile.
Note down the pages where you found the information.

Age: _____

Education: _____

Family and friends: _____

Topics of interest: _____

Political views: _____

Sexual orientation: _____

Black identity (appearance, language, etc.): _____

Character traits: _____

PART 3 (PP. 28–53): TWITTERLUDE 3–5 AND IRL

11

a) Name and describe Method #4 in your own words.

_____

_____

b) Describe the tone of the responses to Method #4.

_____

_____

--- Info ---

Blackface

The term "blackface" is used to refer to the practice of non-black performers wearing theatrical make-up to represent a caricature of black people on stage. This performance tradition was a popular form of entertainment in the US and Britain from around 1830 until the mid-20th century – especially in minstrel shows (for more information cf. the article on pp. 83–84). Today, it is regarded as highly offensive and racist.

c) By wanting Kylie to walk around in "whiteface" (p. 28), Cleo is referring to the term "blackface". Discuss whether the two terms can be compared.

12

In a video by the Darlinghurst Theatre Company, Dr Kathomi Gatwiri, a senior academic, researcher and psychotherapist, is talking about the term "gaslighting". **Webcode** DSW-73699-07

a) Watch the first part of Episode 1: "Racial Gaslighting" (00:00–03:23). Decide whether the following sentences are right or wrong. Correct the wrong statements.

statement	right	wrong	correction
1. Gaslighting is a form of physical abuse.			
2. People who are being gaslighted know that they are being manipulated and are therefore confident about their knowledge.			
3. The term refers to a movie in which a husband makes his wife think that she is just imagining the dimming of lights.			
4. Racial gaslighting is when people of colour are told that their experiences are acknowledged.			

statement	right	wrong	correction
5. Racial gaslighting is deliberately used to maintain white supremacy.			
6. The more people of colour resist to this racial hierarchy the more acceptance they are experiencing in society.			

b) Explain Cleo's accusation: "My own bredrin gaslighting me!" (p. 32)

13

Which sentences about Kara's and Cleo's past are correct? Give proof from the text. → **S23:** How to quote

The primary school teachers admired Cleo's curly hair.   Cleo was always in Kara's shadow.

Cleo had many boyfriends when she was young.   Kara is satisfied with her appearance.

Cleo accuses Kara of not having helped her at a party.

14

a) Name and describe Method #5.

_____

b) Describe the tweets responding to Cleo's Method #5. What historical references are made? (Twitterludes 4 and 5)

_____

PART 4 (PP. 54–78): TWITTERLUDE 6–11 AND IRL

15

a) Cleo's tweets get out of hand when one of her older tweets is retweeted by someone else.
   • What gets retweeted and why?

_____

   • How does Cleo respond?

_____

b) **Pair work** Both Cleo and Kara share stories from the past to explain when they felt misunderstood by each other.
   • **Partner A:** Outline Cleo's story of #wiggate (pp. 45–48).
   • **Partner B:** Outline Kara's story of "T'Sharn's 13th birthday party" (p. 66).
   • Give feedback on how well the summary was performed by your partner.

c) CHALLENGE Comment on the following statement: "If they had acted differently in the past, their relationship now would be a different one." Justify your answer.

d) Name and describe Method #6.

_____

e) Put these events into the right order:

☐ Cleo's identity in real life is revealed on Twitter.

☐ Cleo's IRL and Twitter identities merge into one.

☐ Cleo and Kara have a fight about Cleo's behaviour at T'Sharn's birthday party.

☐ Cleo is blocked from following Kara on Twitter.

☐ Someone retweets a comment by Cleo accusing her of being homophobic.

☐ Cleo apologizes for the two homophobic tweets from 2014.

f) In Method #7, Cleo wants Kylie Jenner to experience the same mistreatments that Saartjie must have gone through. Which mistreatments does Cleo mean? Describe the historical context Cleo is referring to.

_____

_____

_____

THE END (PP. 79–83): THE POST-MORTEM
16
a) With the sentence "I just don't wanna feel heavy no more" (p. 79) Cleo describes a burden she is carrying. From what burden does Cleo need to be freed?

_____

b) Saartjie's spirit is appearing. What are Kara and Cleo praising her for?

_____

c) The image from The Premeditation of Cleo and Kara standing over a body reappears in The Post-Mortem.

Why do you think Jasmine Lee-Jones chose The Post-Mortem as the title for the last scene?

─────────────────────── Info ───────────────────────

Post-mortem (= "after death") refers to the time after a person has died. The term can also be applied to the post-mortem examination of a corpse in order to determine the cause of death.

Post-reading

Relationships
17
a) Describe the friendship between Kara and Cleo. Start a table like the one below.

Help Look at the following pages: 7–9, 21–25, 32–40, 48–49, 59–60, 66, 69–73, 79ff.

section	content	description of their friendship / relationship

b) In the following quote Cleo makes a reference to slavery on a plantation:

"Back in the old days I'd be the field nigger out shucking corn and you'd be in the house beating the master." (p. 39)

71

- Explain the parallels she is drawing.
- What does the quote reveal about the friendship between Cleo and Kara?

c) Kara blocks Cleo from following @KARA and viewing her tweets. Describe Cleo's reaction.
   How would you feel if your best friend did that to you?

d) **Pair work** At the end of the play, Cleo and Kara share a spiritual encounter with Saartjie.
   - Does this experience strengthen their friendship?
   - Discuss: Will they stay friends?

18 Group work   CHOOSE

Create five freeze-frames in which you show the development of Kara and Cleo's relationship. You may act between the freeze-frames.
OR
Choose a part of Cleo and Kara's conversation on pp. 32–35. Act out the scene.

19 Pair work

Talk for five minutes about the question in the bubble and come to a conclusion.

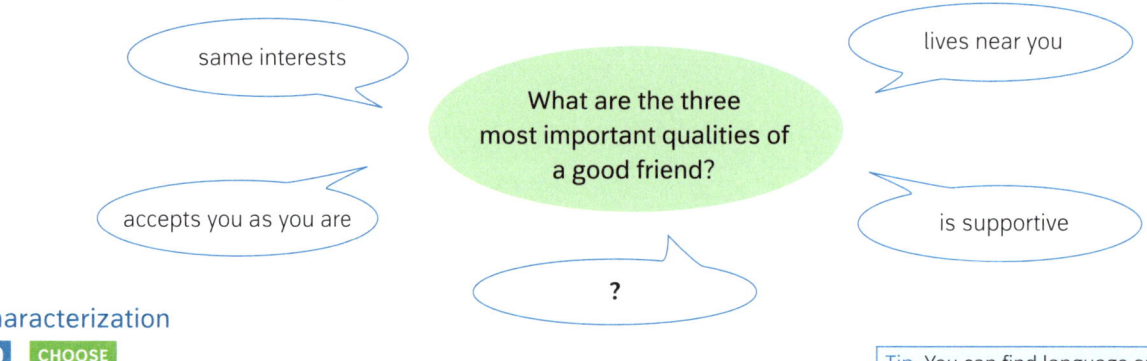

same interests

lives near you

What are the three most important qualities of a good friend?

accepts you as you are

is supportive

?

Characterization

20   CHOOSE

Write a characterization of Cleo (including her online and offline identity)
OR
Kara.
Consider the question of whether Cleo's and/or Kara's character develop throughout the play. Illustrate and prove your answers with the text.   → **Workshop:** Analysing characters   → **S23:** How to quote

> Tip You can find language support for writing a characterization in your textbook *Camden Town Oberstufe* on page 353.

Illustrations and graphic layout of the play's script

21

a) On social media, words are often flanked by photos, emojis, cartoons, etc. Look at the following pages: 4, 10, 12, 13, 17, 44. Explain the combined use of language and pictures in the Twittersphere.
   Start a table like the one below and fill in your findings.
   - Define the type of picture. Is it a photo, a film still, an emoji, a gif, a meme, a cartoon, …?
   - What are the pictures showing?
   - How are pictures used to transport meaning?

Page	Type of picture	What does it show?	Why is it used? What is the meaning?
p. 4			

b) Find more examples and add them to your table.
c) **CHALLENGE** Describe the layout and the way some words are written. What could be the reason why people use such a layout?

_____

_____

d) **CHALLENGE** There are parts in the play where the Twittersphere seems to intersect with real life, e.g. pictures are shown IRL (pp. 22, 34, 45, 71–73). What could be the playwright's intention?

Putting the play on stage

22

A theatre director decides how elements of a play script can be transferred to the stage.

a) **Group work** Come up with an option for how the Twittersphere could be staged. Consider how light, sound, actors, props, stage and audience can play a role.

b) Watch the video of a theatre production. **Webcode** DSW-73699-08
Note down how the scene is staged. Explain the effect on the audience.

c) Take a look at the production photos from the version staged at the Royal Court Theatre in London.
Webcode DSW-73699-09 Considering the elements on stage (ropes, purple-blue cloud, dark background) and the actors' gestures, what part of the play could be shown?

VIPs

23

Cleo and Kara make references to various famous people and characters.

> Joanne the Scammer | Cardi B | Angela Davis | Maxine Waters | MLK | Saartjie (Sarah Baartman)

a) **Group work** Placemat: Work in groups using the placemat method:
- Each group member finds out about one person.
- Write your findings into your section of the placemat.
- Turn the placemat clockwise so that you can read your teammates' findings.
- Discuss and agree on a result, which you write into the group section in the middle.
- Present your results in front of the class.

b) Discuss: To what extent are these people important for the context of the play?

Body images

24

a) **CHOOSE** Choose a country (Iran, Japan, New Zealand, Brazil, France, Kenya, South Korea, Mauritania, Oman or United States) and prepare a two-minute talk on the beauty standard of this country as it is described in the video "How beauty standards differ around the world". **Webcode** DSW-73699-10

b) Who defines what beauty is? Read the extract from an online article from *Medical News Today*. Then explain the quote below in the context of body image as it is described in the article.

What is body image?

By Yvette Brazier *Updated on May 25, 2023*

– Medically reviewed by Marney A. White, PhD, MS, Psychology

Body image refers to how an individual sees their body and their feelings with this perception. Positive body image relates to body satisfaction, while negative body image relates to dissatisfaction.
5 Many people have concerns about their body image. These concerns often focus on weight, skin, hair, or the shape or size of a certain body part. The way a person feels about their body can be influenced by many different factors. According to 10 the National Eating Disorder Association (NEDA), a range of beliefs, experiences, and generalizations contribute to body image.
Throughout history, people have given importance to the beauty of the human body. Society, media, 15 social media, and popular culture often shape these views, and this can affect how a person sees their own body.
However, popular standards are not always helpful.

Constant bombardment by media images and
20 social pressure can cause people to feel uncomfortable about their body, leading to distress and ill health. It can also affect work, social life, and other aspects of life. [...]

What does body image mean?
25 Body image refers to a person's emotional attitudes, beliefs, and perceptions of their own body. Experts describe it as a complex emotional experience.

Body image relates to:
30 • what a person believes about their appearance
• how they feel about their body, height, weight, and shape
• how they sense and experience their body
Positive body image is related to body satisfaction
35 and acceptance, while negative body image is related to dissatisfaction and wanting one's body to be different.
A negative body image can contribute to body dysmorphic disorder (BDD), eating disorders, and
40 other conditions. [...]

"[...] and even Miss Fitzgerald always said how pretty your hair was, and the only time she came remotely close to commenting on how nice my hair was, was when my Mum straightened it for the Year 5 pictures." (p. 35)

25   Pair work
Now take a look at the photo of a woman in front of a mirror by Carrie Mae Weems.
Webcode DSW-73699-11 What does she want to show the viewer about black body image / ethnic identity? Explain.

"I keep a scrapbook with pictures for everything that I write. The main image is currently [art by Carrie Mae Weems] of a black woman looking in the mirror saying "Mirror, mirror on the wall, who's the fairest of them all?" and the mirror's response is "Snow White, you black bitch." That's very much this play."

Jasmine Lee-Jones

Elements and structure of a play
26   → **S11:** How to work with drama

stage directions | scene | characters |
title | setting | playwright | text | cast

a) Label the following elements of a play script.

seven methods of killing kylie jenner ←———— 1. _____

by Jasmine Lee-Jones ←———— 2. _____

———— 3. _____

Cleo a.k.a @INCOGNEGRO   Leanne Henlon
Kara   Tia Bannon ←———— 4. _____

1. ←———— 5. _____

5th March 2019. 4:01AM. ←———— 6. _____
The bird expands and suddenly we are on Twitter.

[...]

Suddenly a figure enters lurking. She creeps on CLEO; touches her.
CLEO jumps. ←———— 7. _____

KARA: (*In a roadman lilt.*) Fuck are you on blad! ←———— 8. _____

b) The development of the plot of a play usually follows a certain structure as shown below.

- Does Jasmine Lee-Jones's play meet this scheme?
- Where can you see contemporary elements?

Tip You can find an explanation of the different terms in your textbook *Camden Town Oberstufe* on page 350.

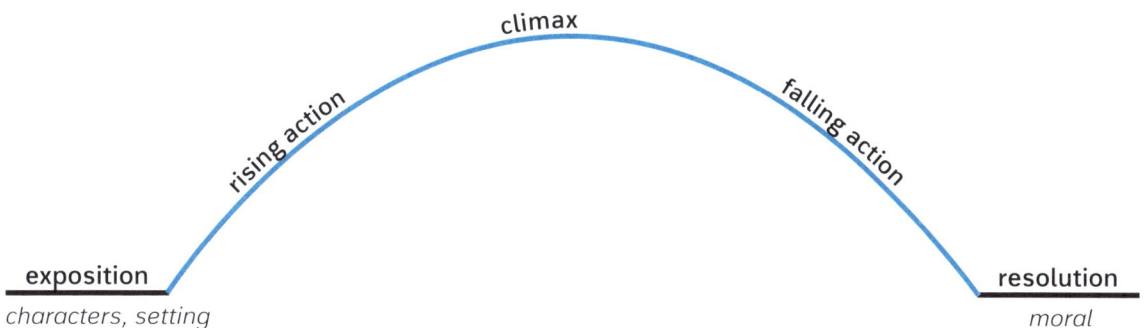

exposition — *characters, setting*
rising action
climax
falling action
resolution — *moral*

Identities

 27

a) Cleo is a black woman having an identity in real life and in the world of Twitter (@INCOGNEGRO). For both identities, her ethnic identity seems to play a role.
How are these identities connected?

identity in real life
ethnic identity
identity in the world of Twitter

b) Choose one of the quotes below and explain it in the context of the conversation between Cleo and Kara.

"You don't own blackness just because you're dark-skinned!" (p. 37)

"You're a lightie." (p. 33)

"All the BW considered universally beautiful are lighties." (p. 34)

Stating your opinion

28 → **S6:** How to write a discussion/comment → **S9:** How to structure a text → **S8:** How to improve your text

Cleo shows her anger by creating hypothetical death threats against Kylie Jenner.

a) CHOOSE
Write a comment on the question of whether you think social media is a good channel to state your opinion.
OR
Pair work Write a digital text together with a partner in a collaborative document.

Help Alternative options to state your opinion and make it public:
- taking part in a demonstration
- talking to people face-to-face
- sending emails or letters to the government or to a newspaper
- starting a petition

b) Why did the playwright choose to include Twitter in her play?

Reviews

29

a) Jasmine Lee-Jones created a contemporary theatre play that has been widely reviewed. Compare the two extracts of reviews by Kate Wyver and Natasher Beecher.

[…] Although the physicalisation of the internet is imaginative, the Twitter-interlude structure feels a little trapped towards the end, as if it's stopped inventing. The arguments begin to circle and the finale can't quite hold the weight of history it attempts to. Nevertheless, Henlon[1] and Bannon[2] are gripping throughout. Jones is a brilliant, dynamic writer, and this is a striking debut.

_____

Kate Wyver: "Seven Methods of Killing Kylie Jenner review – sharp, furious and funny." In: *The Guardian*, 23.06.2021

Annotations
[1] **Leanne Henlon** acted Cleo's part in *seven methods of killing kylie jenner* at the Royal Court Theatre.
[2] **Tia Bannon** acted Kara's part in *seven methods of killing kylie jenner* at the Royal Court Theatre.

[…] For us black women '*seven methods of killing kylie jenner*' with its blend of nostalgia and heart, is us being seen and being heard in a way that's *almost* too difficult to watch, our collective trauma laid bare.

For anyone who isn't black, and white people, in particular, this play will resonate with you in a magical way that you won't quite understand. But one thing is for sure, this poignant play that goes beyond just the zeitgeist is for everyone. It's a play for now and for after – a cultural marker of the way the world is changing and needs to change. Everyone should go see it.

_____

Natasher Beecher: "seven methods of killing kylie jenner review: 'This is one of the best plays I've ever seen'." In: Sophia A Jackson (ed.): *Afridiziak Theatre News*, 23.06.2021

b) **CHOOSE**

Write a review as a tweet.

OR

Write a review for a broadsheet newspaper.

_____

_____

_____

_____

_____

_____

_____

c) Discuss the potential of the play to capture new audiences. Refer back to the article on p. 62. The following questions might give you some inspiration:

- Are you emotionally attached to the play?
- For what reasons would/wouldn't you watch the play?
- Does this play reach all audiences?
- What does it need to attract audiences to the theatre?

The changing media landscape: traditional and modern media

1

Read the short extract from *The Cambridge Introduction to Theatre Studies* and look at the cartoons.
What challenges does the theatre face today? Refer to the material given below.

Theatre and media

by Christopher B. Balme

As one of the oldest media, theatre has survived several epochal shifts in media technology. Whether it was the invention of the printing press or the challenges posed by the invention of cinema, radio or television, 5 the theatre met these innovations with openness and accommodation rather than with rejection. Very often, the new medium took the theatre as its model (with respect to presenting entertainment, especially of the fictional kind (dramatic stories)) 10 before developing other forms and conventions. The theatre always reciprocated by integrating certain elements of the new medium into its own aesthetic and even organizational forms.

[...] the theatre has been exposed to competition from 15 other media since the beginning of the twentieth century, and has certainly lost its previous dominant position as the main purveyor of fictionalized entertainment, [...].

2

Have a look at the website of the Royal Court Theatre in London.   **Webcode**   DSW-73699-12
Summarize the purpose of the theatre and the goals that are named.

The impact of the media on the individual and society

3

a) **Pair work** Brainstorming: List advantages and disadvantages of using social media.

b) Explain the chart. → **S18:** How to analyse statistics

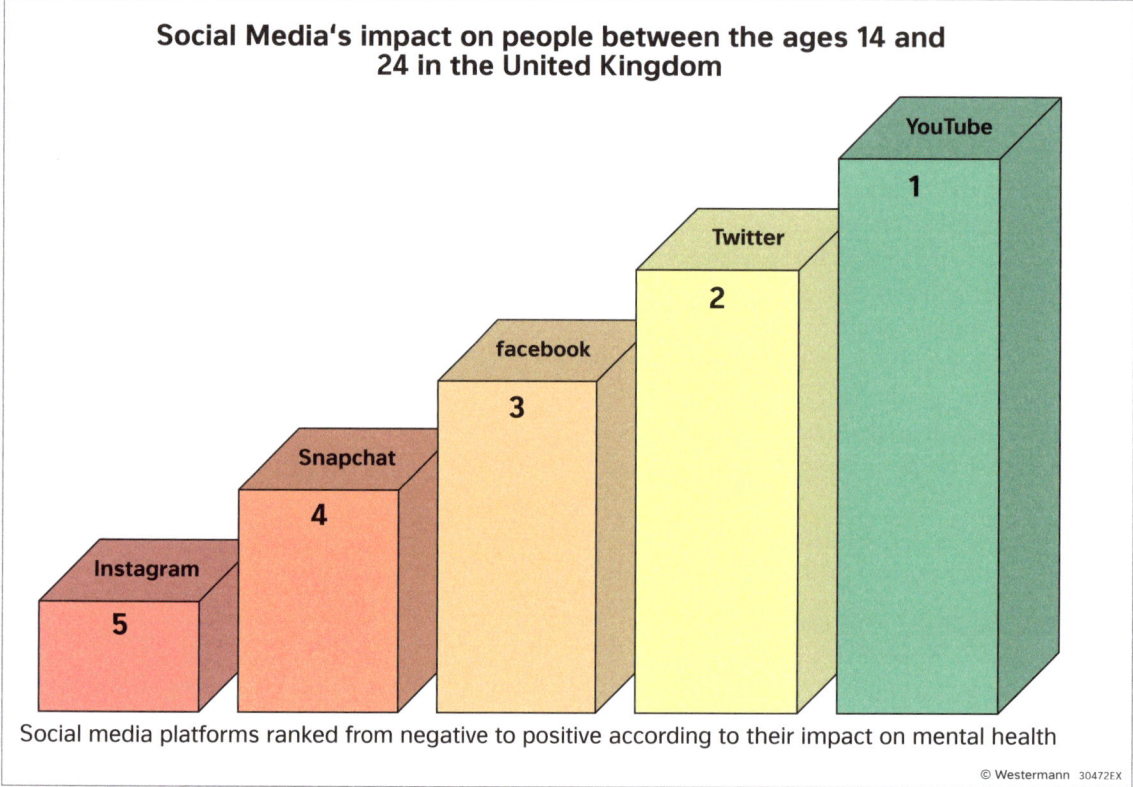

Social Media's impact on people between the ages 14 and 24 in the United Kingdom

YouTube 1
Twitter 2
facebook 3
Snapchat 4
Instagram 5

Social media platforms ranked from negative to positive according to their impact on mental health

© Westermann 30472EX

c) **Pair work** Discuss: Would you take part in a school challenge for a social media free week?

4

Tweets play a major role in *seven methods of killing kylie jenner* and are responsible for the development of the play.

a) Examine to what extent the comments on Twitter change over the course of the play. Use key words to fill in the table.

Content of the Twitterludes	Who is writing?	Scale of factual information (1 true to 9 false)	Scale of humour (1 little to 9 the most)	Scale of hatred (1 little to 9 the most)
1				
2				

Content of the Twitterludes	Who is writing?	Scale of factual information (1 true to 9 false)	Scale of humour (1 little to 9 the most)	Scale of hatred (1 little to 9 the most)
3				
4				
5				
6				
7				
8				
9				
10				
11				

b) Choose adjectives from the box to describe the development and use a timeline/graph/colour scheme to illustrate it.

> accusing | amused | conspirational | funny | homophobic | inflammatory | international | irritated | misogynist | racist | sexist | shocked | surprised

c) With the increasing usage of digital technologies, a new form of bullying has emerged: "cyberbullying". Have you or your friends ever experienced cyberbullying? Describe your experiences (topics, feelings, consequences).

d) **Pair work** At what point in the development of the Twitterludes do you think cyberbullying starts? Give reasons.

5

Cleo and Kara are having a discussion about possible reactions to the death threats against Cleo that are announced on the TL (pp. 43–44).

a) List their arguments. Give your opinion.

b) Cleo describes the following humiliating incident. What is happening?

> "[...] Camera's flashing without my consent
> Over and over
> Images posted all over socials
> Me a meme
> A silent, unconsenting gif
> Like I was some sort of spectacle
> Or a fucking freak
> I've never felt so ugly in my life [...]." (p. 48)

c) Taking photos – now and fifty years ago: What has changed? What role does social media play today?

d) Internet research: Find out about the rules of taking photographs in public and private areas in Germany. Present your findings to the class.

Mediation

6 → **S19:** How to improve your mediation skills

a) Read the 2021 article from *Deutschlandfunk*.

b) Write an email to the playwright Jasmine Lee-Jones in which you describe the latest development in Germany concerning the influence of social media on politics. Refer to her play by pointing out parallels.

Anfeindungen gegen Sarah-Lee Heinrich
Medienexpertin: Koordinierte Twitter-Kampagnen als Methode

Immer häufiger werden Akteure aus Politik und Medien im Netz mit fragwürdigen Aussagen aus ihrer Vergangenheit konfrontiert. Dabei gerate aus dem Blick, aus welchen Kreisen diese Enthüllungen stammen, sagte Tajana Graovac vom „No Hate Speech Movement" im Dlf.

Sarah-Lee Heinrich

Ein paar Tweets können reichen, damit bei Twitter und darüber hinaus innerhalb weniger Stunden eine große Debatte in Gang kommt. So war das zuletzt zum Beispiel im Fall der neuen Bundessprecherin der Grünen Jugend.

Sarah-Lee Heinrich geriet in den Fokus wegen mehrerer alter Nachrichten, in denen sie im Jahr 2015 zum Beispiel „Heil" unter einen Tweet mit
20 Hakenkreuz geschrieben hatte. Die heute 20-Jährige schrieb, sie könne sich nicht daran erinnern, als Jugendliche jemals einen solchen Tweet abgesetzt zu haben.

„Das war maximal dumm und unangebracht",
25 schrieb Heinrich. Die Sozialwissenschafts-Studentin betonte aber auch, dass sie sich „jetzt nicht zu allem erklären" wolle, „was ich mal so mit 14 gedacht und gesagt habe".

Erst Tweets, dann Morddrohungen
30 Heinrich beklagte außerdem, seit ihrer Wahl versuchten Rechte, Shitstorms gegen sie hochzuziehen: „Haben wohl Bammel vor einer schwarzen, linken Frau", schrieb Heinrich.
Nach diesen Tweets zog sich Heinrich vorerst aus
35 der Öffentlichkeit zurück. Der Grünen-Jugendorganisation zufolge hatte sie Mord- und Gewaltandrohungen erhalten. Es gehe „jetzt erst einmal darum, alles für ihre Sicherheit zu tun", sagte der scheidende Bundessprecher der Grünen Jugend,
40 Georg Kurz.

„Das ist koordiniert"
Dass der Fall eine solche Entwicklung genommen hat, sei typisch, sagte Tajana Graovac vom „No Hate Speech Movement" im Deutschlandfunk.
45 „Was wir feststellen können, dass es große Accounts sind, die meistens eher in der rechten Ecke zu finden sind, die große Reichweite haben", sagte Graovac.
Accounts aus rechten und rechtsextremen Kreisen
50 würden dann dafür sorgen, dass sich die entsprechenden Nachrichten weit verbreiten. „Das ist koordiniert. Und es ist tatsächlich auch immer das gleiche Schema und das geht fast immer nach der gleichen Dynamik", so Graovac weiter.

55 **Manipulierte Kampagnen erkennen**
Zudem würden zum Teil Screenshots verbreitet, die nachträglich manipuliert worden seien. „Man schneidet die Zeit und das Datum ab, damit die irgendwie auch aktuell aussehen. Es werden teilweise
60 Wörter weggelassen, damit die Tweets noch schlimmer klingen. Und das zieht dann wirklich Kreise."
Aufgabe von Journalistinnen und Journalisten sei es, dies zu erkennen und nicht auf eine Kampagne hereinzufallen. Sie müssten offenlegen, „dass es
65 eine gezielte, koordinierte Attacke ist gegen eine schwarze Person".

Stereotypes and images of black female identity

7 → **S17:** How to work with cartoons

a) Study the depiction of the woman carefully. Then describe the cartoon.

Language support

index finger | megaphone | speech bubble

b) Explain the message of the cartoon by referring to its individual elements.

c) Come up with a possible title and give reasons for your decision.

d) Black women have often been depicted in the media and society as 'angry', 'aggressive' and 'sassy'. Think of situations in which black women could be seen as behaving in an "angry" way.

e) Read an article about this stereotype from an online encyclopedia.

Webcode DSW-73699-13

Use key words to sum up the text. Compare your result with a partner.

f) Discuss how it is possible for black women to escape the vicious circle of being referred to as an "angry black woman" when they show anger about being called this term.
You may refer to Michelle Obama's reactions described in the following extract from a 2012 article from the *BBC*.

Michelle Obama: 'I'm no angry black woman'

US First Lady Michelle Obama has challenged a new book's account of her role in the White House, saying critics have long attempted to portray her as "some kind of angry black woman".

The Obamas, by New York Times reporter Jodi Kantor, portrays her as a behind-the-scenes force in the White House. [...]
While she pushed back against the notion she
5 sits in political meetings, Mrs Obama did not deny being an important voice to her husband.
"I am his biggest ally," Mrs Obama said. "I am one of his biggest confidants. But he has dozens of really smart people who surround him. That's
10 not to say that we don't have discussions and conversations.

"I guess it's more interesting to imagine this conflicted situation here and a strong woman. But that's been an image that people have tried to
15 paint of me since the day Barack announced [he would run for president] – that I'm some angry black woman," she said.
"I just try to be me. And my hope is that over time people get to know me," she told CBS. "And they
20 get to judge me for me." [...]

8

Read the 2018 article from the *BBC*.

Outline the views on the stereotype of the "angry black woman" as presented in this article.

Serena Williams and the trope of the 'angry black woman'

By Ritu Prasad   *11 September 2018*

Mammies, jezebels, Sapphires. Black women in America have long been dogged by negative stereotypes, rooted in a history of racism and slavery. In the aftermath of Serena Williams'
5 **controversial US Open loss, it's the trope[1] of the "angry black woman" that has once again re-emerged.**

During the US Open final, Williams received a code violation for coaching[2], a penalty point for breaking
10 her racquet and a game penalty for calling the umpire a "thief". And later, a fine of $17,000 (£13,000). Her reactions to the referee's calls – which the Women's Tennis Association has since decried as "sexist" – were no different from how many top
15 players react in the heat of a championship game. But it was the way she was punished for her anger that has sparked further outrage.

"As it was unfolding I could tell this was not going to turn out well," says law professor Trina Jones.
20 "I knew it was going to be a trainwreck." In addition to being a long-time tennis fan, Prof Jones has studied racial stereotyping and how it plays into the lives of African-American women. "Black women are not supposed to push back and
25 when they do, they're deemed to be domineering. Aggressive. Threatening. Loud." Similar words have been levelled[3] at Serena Williams more than once, as well as former First Lady Michelle Obama and top Democrat Maxine
30 Waters in recent years. Williams has been docked before for her behaviour on the court – in 2009, she was fined $82,500 for an angry outburst – though she is far from the only player to face punishment for similar conduct.
35 Prof Jones says some have compared the referee's calls to speeding tickets: many people speed and sometimes a few are caught. But that analogy, she says, misses the point that African Americans are disproportionately pulled
40 aside. In the case of Williams, she was first dinged[4] on a coaching violation that happens often but is rarely called out as the player's fault. "Why would a black woman in a championship match therefore be called on it?" Prof Jones says,
45 adding that an attack on one's integrity is only natural to be angry about. "[Williams] is outraged because she knows the context."

The myth of the 'angry black woman'

50 The "angry black woman" trope has its roots in 19th Century America, when minstrel shows, which involved comic skits[5] and variety acts, mocking African Americans became popular. Blair Kelley, associate professor of history at North
55 Carolina State University, says black women were often played by overweight white men who painted their faces black and donned fat suits "to make them look less than human, unfeminine, ugly". "Their main way of interacting with the men around
60 them was to scream and fight and come off angry, irrationally so, in response to the circumstances around them," she says. The 1930s programme *Amos 'n' Andy* was one of the first modern media portrayals to cement this
65 stereotype through the character of Mrs Sapphire Stevens. "The real problem in their everyday life was not the structural things that black people faced, but the mouth of the black woman – her tone, her
70 irrationality and her anger," Prof Kelley says of Sapphire's role. As segregation laws known as Jim Crow laws saw black Americans assaulted, jailed and killed, popular culture pushed ideas of "sassy[6] mammies"
75 and "Sapphires" – an archetype depicting black women with iron-fists, yelling at everyone from children to white men. This trope of the "angry black woman" has endured, and has been pervasive[7] in modern
80 media even without more overtly racist portrayals, says Brandi Collins, senior campaign director at

---

Annotations

1 **trope** = *Tropus, bildlicher Ausdruck*
2 **coaching** = Players aren't allowed to be coached in Grand Slam matches. Violations lead to warnings or penalties.
3 **to be levelled at** = to be aimed or directed at sb or sth

4 **to ding** = to make a ringing sound (like a bell); to criticize sb
5 **comic skit** = a short, funny play
6 **sassy** = *frech*
7 **pervasive** = present, noticeable, widespread

the racial justice organisation Color of Change. On screen, it is easy to push sass for laughs. But black women in America see these depictions
85 translate differently in real life.

For Ms Collins, the picture of the "hyperemotional" black woman has become more commonplace as Americans grapple[8] with issues of polarised politics and civility.

90 Black women, she says, are often faced with people responding to their emotions "from a place of perceived fear".

"There's almost a paranoia around it. A feeling that you have to go above and beyond to make people
95 feel comfortable around you."

In a 2016 interview with Oprah Winfrey, former First Lady Michelle Obama echoed the same sentiment. "You think, that is so not me! But then you sort of think, well, this isn't about me," she said of being
100 labelled as an "angry black woman".

"This is about the person or the people who write it … We are so afraid of each other, you know?"

Robin Boylorn, an intercultural communications professor at the University of Alabama told the
105 BBC it seems impossible to be a black woman and not be angry, after "generations of oppression, discrimination and erasure".

"Black women should be celebrated for not being completely consumed by anger," she says.

110 "Men are allowed to be angry as a performance of masculinity. White women are allowed to be angry as a clarion call[9]. So black women should be encouraged to express their anger as well, particularly in the face of injustice."

115 For Serena Williams, Prof Boylorn says the issue is compounded by the fact that "she cannot separate her blackness from her womanhood, from her class or social status".

But it's the double standard with men in particular
120 that has come up in the ongoing debate of Williams' US Open performance.

In a cartoon that went viral after the final, Williams is drawn as a petulant, mannish figure while the referee tells her opponent, "Can you just let her win?"
125 "It's indicative of the way in which Serena has been, throughout her career, treated both by media and within US tennis as angry, unhinged, really aggressive," says Ms Collins of Color of Change.

"When you see her be degraded or treated in that
130 way, it really can lead young black girls and girls in general to question whether or not they should be the full range of what it means to be a woman."

But Ms Collins notes that fixing the problem is not just about eliminating the "angry black woman" trope.
135 "For every type of white man you can imagine, there's a movie about his story and his experience and his journey. Black women in media aren't afforded that diversity of experience," she says.

Instead, understanding
140 the diversity of a black woman's experience – and not just her anger – is key. For Williams, that's a lesson she hopes her fans
145 will learn from her US Open upset.

"I'm here to fight for women's rights and women's equality.
150 The fact that I have to go through this is an example," she told reporters after the match.

"Maybe it didn't work
155 out for me, but it's going to work out for the next person."

Annotations
8 to **grapple** = to try to deal with sth
9 **clarion call** = *Weckruf*

9

Explain why it is inadequate to refer to an African-American woman as an "angry black woman".

_____

_____

_____

_____

_____

_____

_____

_____

_____

_____

Looking back at the play

10 Pair work

Cleo is being criticized for her behaviour on the TL, e.g. "I for one can't believe @INCOGNEGRO acting like dis. U ain't the next civil rights activist!" (p. 19).

Are there any more parallels between Serena Williams' depiction as an "angry black woman" and the comments on Twitter that describe Cleo as hysterical and overreacting?

_____

_____

_____

_____

_____

_____

_____

_____

_____

11 Group work

Your school is planning a project week with the topic "school for the future" and is asking students to send in podcasts, videos, posters, etc. with ideas about how schools can address and eliminate racism. What would be your contribution? Visualize your ideas.

TEXTQUELLEN

6–7　Kate Chopin: "The Story of an Hour." (Original title: "The Dream of an Hour.") In: *Vogue*, 6 December 1894.

9　Quote from Kate Chopin: "The Story of an Hour." (Original title: "The Dream of an Hour.") In: *Vogue*, 6 December 1894.

10–17　Fay Weldon: "Weekend." In: *Cosmopolitan*, 1978.

21–23　Bernardine Evaristo: "The First Feminists." Holly Fraser (ed.), Amsterdam: WePresent/WeTransfer, 09.04.2020. https://wepresent.wetransfer.com/stories/literally-bernardine-evaristo (05.09.2023)

24–25　Quotes from Bernardine Evaristo: "The First Feminists." Holly Fraser (ed.), Amsterdam: WePresent/WeTransfer, 09.04.2020. https://wepresent.wetransfer.com/stories/literally-bernardine-evaristo (05.09.2023)

25　Quotes from Kate Chopin: "The Story of an Hour." (Original title: "The Dream of an Hour.") In: *Vogue*, 6 December 1894.

25　Quotes from Fay Weldon: "Weekend." In: *Cosmopolitan*, 1978.

27　Infographic: Medical Model | Social Model. Windsor, New South Wales, Australia: EPIC Assist/EPIC Employment Inc. https://epicassistau.b-cdn.net/wp-content/uploads/2021/07/Medical-model-vs-social.png (12.12.2023) (verändert)

28　Paul Sloane: "The Dangers of Conformity." London: BBN Times, 24.07.2023. https://www.bbntimes.com/politics/the-dangers-of-conformity (13.12.2023)

29　Quote by Gloria Steinem: "A gender-equal society ..." In: Praneta Jha: "Feminism makes love easier, says Gloria Steinem." In: *Hindustan Times*, 18.01.2014. https://www.hindustantimes.com/india/feminism-makes-love-easier-says-gloria-steinem/story-CMt7gY31ffRlpYcfetbvBL.html (14.12.2023)

31　Quotes from Emmaline Soken-Huberty: "10 Causes of Gender Inequality." Wien: Human Rights Careers. https://www.humanrightscareers.com/issues/causes-gender-inequality/ (14.12.2023) (verändert)

31 f.　„Gemeinsame Doppelnamen reichen nicht!" Ein Kommentar von Tanja Dückers. Köln: Deutschlandfunk Kultur/Deutschlandradio, 03.04.2023. https://www.deutschlandfunkkultur.de/heirat-nachname-meshing-100.html (14.12.2023)

34　Dictionary entry: "behold". In: *Oxford Languages*. Oxford: Oxford University Press 2023.

38–55　Quotes from Imbolo Mbue: *Behold the Dreamers*. New York: Random House (Penguin Random House LLC) 2016.

39　"Bankruptcy of Lehman Brothers." In: *Britannica*. Chicago, IL: Encyclopædia Britannica, Inc. 2023. https://www.britannica.com/event/bankruptcy-of-Lehman-Brothers (07.11.2023)

43 ff.　Aaron Bady: "Has Imbolo Mbue Written the Great American Novel?" New York: *Literary Hub*, 26.10.2016. https://lithub.com/has-imbolo-mbue-written-the-great-american-novel/ (08.11.2023)

45 ff.　Annabelle Hirsch: „So hat Amerika die Einwanderer immer gebraucht." In: *Frankfurter Allgemeine Zeitung*, 11.02.2017. https://www.faz.net/aktuell/feuilleton/buecher/rezensionen/roman-das-getraeumte-land-von-imbolo-mbue-14873429.html (09.11.2023)

48　Quote from James Truslow Adams: *The Epic of America*. Boston: Little, Brown and Company 1931.

48, 51　Quote from the *United States Declaration of Independence*, In Congress, July 4, 1776. Washington, D.C.: The U.S. National Archives and Records Administration 2023. https://www.archives.gov/founding-docs/declaration-transcript (13.11.2023)

48　Quote from Malcolm X (el-Hajj Malik el-Shabazz): "The Ballot or the Bullet." Speech given in Detroit on April 12, 1964. St. Paul, Minnesota: American Public Media 2023. https://americanradioworks.publicradio.org/features/blackspeech/mx.html (13.11.2023)

48　Quote by George Carlin: "The reason they call it the American Dream ..." In: Kelly Carlin: "George Carlin: Every American Dreams." Washington, DC: National Portrait Gallery. https://npg.si.edu/blog/george-carlin-every-american-dreams (13.11.2023)

48　Quote from Michelle Obama: Speech at the Democratic National Convention in Charlotte, N.C. on September 4, 2012. Washington, D.C.: National Public Radio (NPR) 2023. https://www.npr.org/2012/09/04/160578836/transcript-michelle-obamas-convention-speech (13.11.2023)

49　Quotes from Martin Luther King Jr.: "I Have a Dream." Speech delivered during the March on Washington for Jobs and Freedom on August 28, 1963. Washington, D.C.: National Public Radio (NPR) 2023. https://www.npr.org/2010/01/18/122701268/i-have-a-dream-speech-in-its-entirety (13.11.2023)

49　Jeannette L. Nolen: "Equality." In: *Britannica*. Chicago, IL: Encyclopædia Britannica, Inc. 2023. https://www.britannica.com/topic/equality-human-rights (13.11.2023)

49 f.　Catherine Hoffmann: „Die Illusion vom amerikanischen Traum." In: *Süddeutsche Zeitung*, 27.01.2017. https://www.sueddeutsche.de/wirtschaft/soziale-gerechtigkeit-die-illusion-vom-amerikanischen-traum-1.3350589 (13.11.2023)

51　Quote from Carmela Ciuraru: "New Books by Imbolo Mbue, Krys Lee, Gonzalo Torné and Lisa McInerney." In: *The New York Times*, 28.08.2016. https://www.nytimes.com/2016/08/29/books/new-books-by-imbolo-mbue-krys-lee-gonzalo-torne-and-lisa-mcinerney.html?_r=0 (13.11.2023)

53 ff.　Andrew Ross Sorkin: "From Trump to Trade, the Financial Crisis Still Resonates 10 Years Later." In: *The New York Times*, 10.09.2018. From The New York Times. © 2024 The New York Times Company. All rights reserved. Used under license. https://www.nytimes.com/2018/09/10/business/dealbook/financial-crisis-trump.html (09.11.2023)

56 f.　Barack Obama: "The American Promise." Address Accepting the Presidential Nomination at the Democratic National Convention in Denver on August 28, 2008. In: Gerhard Peters and John T. Woolley: The American Presidency Project. Santa Barbara: University of California, Santa Barbara. https://www.presidency.ucsb.edu/documents/address-accepting-the-presidential-nomination-the-democratic-national-convention-denver (14.11.2023)

58　Brian Duignan: "January 6 U.S. Capitol attack." In: *Britannica*. Chicago, IL: Encyclopædia Britannica, Inc. 2023. https://www.britannica.com/event/January-6-U-S-Capitol-attack (14.11.2023)

58　Quote from Lucia Grave: "America's Trump nightmare has arrived." In: *The Guardian*, 04.05.2016. https://www.theguardian.com/commentisfree/2016/may/03/americas-trump-nightmare-has-arrived (14.11.2023)

62 Jessie Thompson: "Jasmine Lee-Jones interview: I want people to come to the theatre like they watch Netflix."
In: *The Standard*, 17.06.2021. © Evening Standard 2024. https://www.standard.co.uk/culture/theatre/
jasmine-lee-jones-seven-methods-of-killing-kylie-jenner-royal-court-london-b940966.html (02.04.2022)

63–85 Quotes from Jasmine Lee-Jones: *seven methods of killing kylie jenner*. London/New York/Dublin:
Methuen Drama/Bloomsbury Publishing Plc 2021.

66 Quote from Jasmine Lee-Jones: *seven methods of killing kylie jenner*. London: Oberon Books/Bloomsbury
Publishing Plc 2019, p. 1.

73f. Yvette Brazier: "What is body image?" In: Robin Hough (ed.): *Medical News Today*, 25.05.2023. Brighton:
Healthline Media UK Ltd. 2024. https://www.medicalnewstoday.com/articles/249190#definition (07.02.2024)

74 Quote by Jasmine Lee-Jones: "I keep a scrapbook with pictures ..." In: Amel Mukhtar: "Meet The 20-Year-
Old Playwright Behind The Provocative Drama 'Seven Methods Of Killing Kylie Jenner'." In: *British Vogue*,
04.07.2019. https://www.vogue.co.uk/article/jasmine-lee-jones-seven-methods-of-killing-kylie-jenner-
interview (04.04.2022)

76 Kate Wyver: "Seven Methods of Killing Kylie Jenner review – sharp, furious and funny." In: *The Guardian*,
23.06.2021. Copyright Guardian News & Media Ltd 2024. https://www.theguardian.com/stage/2021/jun/23/
seven-methods-of-killing-kylie-jenner-review-royal-court (04.04.2022)

76 Natasher Beecher: "seven methods of killing kylie jenner review: 'This is one of the best plays I've ever seen'."
In: Sophia A Jackson (ed.): *Afridiziak Theatre News*, 23.06.2021. http://www.afridiziak.com/reviews/
seven-methods-of-killing-kylie-jenner/ (04.04.2022)

77 Christopher B. Balme: "Theatre and media." In: *The Cambridge Introduction to Theatre Studies*.
Cambridge: Cambridge University Press 2008, p. 195. https://www.cambridge.org/core/books/abs/
cambridge-introduction-to-theatre-studies/theatre-and-media/4829F5F357C29C2E9D28407C0818CC6A
(29.01.2024)

80f. „Anfeindungen gegen Sarah-Lee Heinrich – Medienexpertin: Koordinierte Twitter-Kampagnen als Methode."
Tajana Graovac im Gespräch mit Sebastian Wellendorf. Köln: Deutschlandfunk/Deutschlandradio, 13.10.2021.
https://www.deutschlandfunk.de/anfeindungen-gegen-sarah-lee-heinrich-medienexpertin.2907.
de.html?dram:article_id=504219 (04.04.2022)

82 "Michelle Obama: 'I'm no angry black woman'." London: BBC, 11.01.2012. https://www.bbc.com/news/
world-us-canada-16515834 (23.05.2022)

83f. Ritu Prasad: "Serena Williams and the trope of the 'angry black woman'." London: BBC, 11.09.2018.
https://www.bbc.com/news/world-us-canada-45476500 (04.04.2022)